THE ELEPHANT AND THE FLEA

Reflections of a Reluctant Capitalist

CHARLES HANDY

Harvard Business School Press
Boston, Massachusetts

First published in the United Kingdom in 2001 by Hutchinson
The Random House Group Limited
20 Vauxhall Bridge Road, London SW1V 2SA

Printed in the United States of America
07 06 05 04 03 5 4 3 2 1

Library of Congress Cataloging-in-Publication Data

Handy, Charles B.
    The elephant and the flea : reflections of a reluctant capitalist / Charles Handy.
        p. cm.
    Includes index.
    ISBN 1-57851-822-9 (alk. paper)
        1. Capitalism—Philosophy. 2. Economics—Philosophy. I. Title

HB501.H338 2202
330.12'2—dc21

2001051664

ISBN 1-59139-128-8 (pbk)

CONTENTS

PART I

THE FOUNDATIONS

1

1981: TO START IN THE MIDDLE

I woke up early on the morning of 25 July 1981. It was my forty-ninth birthday. Not usually a landmark event, one might think, but I was drowsily aware that this time the cliché was true; today really was going to be the first day of the rest of my life. In six days' time I would be unemployed – by my own choice. I didn't call it unemployed, of course. I was 'going portfolio' I would say, proudly using the term I had coined a couple of years earlier to describe the kind of life that, I predicted, more and more people would be leading by the end of the century.

It had been foolhardy then, at the start of the Thatcher years in Britain, to prophesy that by the year 2000 less than half of the working population would be in conventional full-time jobs on what are called 'indefinite period contracts'. The rest of us would either be self-employed, or part-timers, perhaps temps of one sort or another, or out of paid work altogether. We would need, I said, a portfolio of different bits and pieces of paid work, or a collection of different clients or customers, if we wanted to earn a living. A full and rich life, however, would be a more complicated portfolio of different categories of work – paid work, gift work, study work or learning, plus, for both men and women, the necessary work in the home, cooking, caring and cleaning. The elusive work/life balance would actually be a mixture of different forms of work, seasoned with a touch of leisure and pleasure.

People scoffed; business executives, politicians and academics, all of them. They mocked my comment that 'househusbands' would be a vogue term by the turn of the century. The Thatcher doctrine of enterprise and self-reliance was supposed to create a booming economy with conventional jobs for all who wanted them. If it failed, well, the alternative of the socialist state would do its best to return us to that happy state of full employment, even if it meant using the state as the employer of last resort. It was a debate about ways of getting to an agreed end. The idea that the desired end, the full-employment society, might not be on the cards in the sense of jobs for all was not worth talking about.

I told the doubters of the forty-eight-year-old advertising account executive who was complaining to me that there were no longer any jobs in the ageist advertising world for people like him. While he was talking to me in my home, the electrician repairing our wiring put his head round the door to say that he would be back, but not for a week. 'I'm sorry,' he said, seeing my face darken with disappointment, 'but I've got too many jobs on at the moment.'

That was the future, I told my account executive; lots of electrician-type jobs, meaning customers and clients for the independent worker, but fewer and fewer of his own type of job where you sold your time in advance, usually years in advance, to an organization.

Like him, people listened but chose not to hear. The employee society of the twentieth century had delivered so much that was good – secure household incomes for most, a convenient tax-collecting mechanism, a way of parcelling society into boxes so that you knew where people were; and so that individuals also knew where they would be, and what they would be doing in the years to come. The career in an organization, even if it changed once or twice in a lifetime, seemed to be the central bond that kept society from degenerating into a selfish battleground, each for himself and herself and devil take the rest. The very different world I foresaw, however, was fraught with insecurity for most, with uncertainty and fear. 'We don't want that sort of world' people said, and hoped that it would not happen. I sympathized. I, too, didn't much like the sort of world that I saw emerging, but wishing it away was not going to help.

I consoled myself with the observation of the philosopher Arthur Schopenhauer that all truth passes through three stages. First it is ridiculed. Second it is opposed. Third it is accepted as being self-evident.

As it turned out, by the year 2000 the British labour force on those indefinite period contracts in full-time employment had fallen to 40 per cent and the BBC World Service was running programmes on the theme 'What Future for Men?' as women seemed to be runnning everything apart from the old corporations and professions. Full employment had been redefined to mean less than 5 per cent of the self-declared workforce claiming benefit. What the rest were doing or not doing was irrelevant. Already, by 1996, in Britain 67 per cent of British businesses had only one employee, the owner, and in 1994 so-called micro-enterprises employing less than five people made up 89 per cent of all businesses. Putting it more starkly, only 11 per cent of businesses employed more than five people.

Back in 1981, however, I had decided that it was not enough to prophecy. I ought to try to practise what I had been preaching, to find out for myself what it felt like to leave the shelter of organizations and fend for myself, to be what I have come to call a flea, outside the world of the elephants, the big organizations that had been the pillars of the employee society of the twentieth century. The fleas are the independent operators, some of them with small businesses of their own, some working by themselves or in a partnership.

Elephants and fleas is an odd metaphor, equally unflattering to both groups. I hit upon it by chance when looking for a way, in a public lecture, to explain why large organizations needed irritant individuals or groups to introduce the innovations and ideas essential to their survival. After the lecture I was struck by the number of people who came up to me, either proclaiming themselves to be a flea or lamenting the ponderous gait of the elephant where they worked. The analogy, it seemed, had caught their imagination, so I persevered with it. Like all analogies, however, it should not be pushed too far. Useful for attracting attention, it is not in itself a recipe for solutions, but as a broad description of one divide in modern society it serves its purpose.

It is, for instance, the elephants who get all the attention while most people actually work as fleas or for a flea organization. There are, as one example, more people working in ethnic restaurants in Britain today than in the steel, coal, shipbuilding and automobile companies put together. Those huge elephants of old have been superceded by flea organizations as the economy moves from manufacturing to services. It is a new world.

It would be a new world for me too, one in which I exchanged security for freedom.

I had been privileged to spend ten years working for one of the largest of the commercial elephants – the Royal Dutch Shell Group – who had marked my first day at work by handing me details of their pension scheme, as a sign of their intention to occupy the whole of my working life. I left them for the equally secure world of a university where 'tenure' at that time meant a guaranteed right to teach until retirement, no matter how radical or out-of-date your views. From there I had left to work in Windsor Castle, where permanence and continuity were part of the very fabric of the place.

So that morning, as I lay in bed, I was looking at the musical notations painted on the walls of my room by a choirmaster in the sixteenth century. I was sleeping in part of what had originally been the thirteenth-century home or palace of Henry III. The rooms had later become the choir school of the Chapel of St George. It was now my temporary home because for the last four years I had been Warden of St George's House, a small conference and study centre in the Castle devoted to the discussion of ethical issues in society and to the preparation of clergy for senior roles in the Churches. The conference room of the centre, I told participants, had once been used for a performance of *The Merry Wives of Windsor*, directed by William Shakespeare himself, in front of Queen Elizabeth I.

When the Clerk of Works of the Castle handed me a great key that entitled me to enter a restricted part of the grounds he asked me to sign for it in a large and venerable leather volume. 'Please be sure to write the year in full,' he said. 'We can get confused between the centuries in this place.' The canons of the Chapel of St George had, until very recently, been granted lifetime freeholds, the right to hold on to their houses and their positions not just until retirement but until they died. Windsor Castle had been around for a very long time and had every intention of staying that way.

As an unchanging rock it had been a good place from which to study the changing world outside, but in 1981 it was time for me to leave its safety and try my fortunes outside, before I became too fossilized to survive there. I had no savings to speak of, a mortgage, a wife, two teenage children and had not been long enough attached to any of my organizations to collect anything resembling a proper pension. Life was going to be a trifle uncertain, I could see, since all I could do was write and talk. Maybe I had been unduly rash, I reflected that morning, to resign so impulsively, just to satisfy the masochistic principle of practising what I preached, to leave the world of the elephants and the big battalions and join the fleas, the lone warriors who, I was predicting, would be the growing population of the future.

Nor had my life until then been the best preparation for the independent existence that I now faced. Indeed, as I looked back on my early upbringing in a rectory in the Irish countryside, my education in the best (or worst?) of the British public school and Oxbridge tradition, and my subsequent work experience in an international company that often seemed to have been modelled on a blend of the British Army and the civil service, I realized that none of them was going to help me with my new challenges. Even the business school that I had helped to form was, I now felt, inappropriately conceived for the world that I believed lay ahead of us all.

That was all twenty years ago. This book is, in part, my very personal reflections on how the world has changed in that time and how it may change yet further and faster in the years ahead, so fast, indeed, that what is a breakthrough as I write may be stale news by the time it is read. Communism was already a failed ideology in 1981 but no one then foresaw the fall of the Berlin Wall and the demise of the Soviet Empire. The result has been a triumphant capitalism that has brought its own dilemmas, giving money a more central role in all our lives than we had previously experienced and changing many of our priorities.

In 1981, Internet and world wide web were terms not heard in our Windsor conversations – indeed, the web was not even a glimmer in the mind of Tim Berners-Lee, the Englishman who ten years later gave it to the world for free – but they became just two of the forces that have transformed life for both fleas and elephants in ways that we could not even dream of twenty years ago, and Berners-Lee is now saying that there are more new excitements on their way. In the light of this experience it might be thought a little hazardous, even ridiculous, to try to gaze a further twenty years into the future. Looking back, however, I think I can argue that these momentous events have only accelerated the possible changes to our lives that we were debating in 1981.

I remember Kingman Brewster, then the American ambassador to the Court of St James, and recently retired as president of Yale University, raising the question in a lecture that year of who would be the trustees of our future. It was a nice, grandiloquent way of querying whether our preoccupation with short-term economic questions both in society and in our own lives might not be blinding us to more fundamental questions about the meaning of success, the kind of society we wanted our grandchildren to inherit, and our own responsibilities for doing something about it. Horizons have shortened still further and economics become even more dominant but the questions still need answering.

I was born in Ireland, then a poor, priest-ridden land, where time seemed elastic and the talk endless. Now it rejoices in its tag of the Celtic Tiger. My native city of Dublin is buzzing but to my eyes it is also a permanent traffic jam whose pollution clouds the air, the people are harassed and lunch is a sandwich at the desk rather than the leisurely affair of old. The Irish, returning now not emigrating, find house prices in the stratosphere, forcing them to live way out of town and to add their own contribution to the daily traffic queues. 'It's not the Ireland we remember,' they lament. 'There's no time for chat, and the suburban sprawl has smothered too many of the old green fields. It's like any other consumer society these days.' Yes, but the people, most of them, have more money to spend. Isn't that good? I'm not sure.

I remember my old economics professor, a Central European who had located himself in America, saying once that it was much more exciting to work in a country where the economy was booming, but that he preferred to live in lands where it was stagnant. 'You can always get a taxi or a seat in a restaurant, the theatre is better and the talk more philosophical, there is time to live.' Progress is a tricky topic, then and now, and I don't suppose that any new technologies will alter the dilemmas.

Those dilemmas may even get more difficult. Somehow, instead of technology and productivity giving us more time for leisure, as we all expected, we seem to be more consumed by work than ever. Work now must not only deliver the means for life but also the point of life for all us workaholics. Can work, most of it, live up to the challenge, or will a successful capitalism ultimately prove to be a great disappointment?

It was already apparent, twenty years ago, that life was getting longer and healthier for most of us and that organizational careers were getting shorter, although no one anticipated American presidents retiring in their fifties after two terms or someone becoming leader of the Tory party in his thirties. Shell had told me, when giving me that pension book back in 1956, that, if past statistics were any guide, I would probably only live to enjoy my pension for eighteen months, and my own father did indeed live for only twenty months after his retirement.

But by 1981 it wasn't eighteen months but eighteen years that loomed for most of us between retirement and death, a gap that wasn't going to be easily filled by endless television, cruises and golf, nor would any conceivable state pension allow us to afford such delights. We adopted the term Third Age to lend the gap an optimistic tinge. But naming something does not mean that we are any closer, today, to knowing what we shall do with that bonus of an extra twenty years or more, or how we shall finance them.

Twenty years ago, too, it was already clear that as corporations got bigger in their reach they would also need to get smaller in their parts. They had to be local, they were saying, in order to be effective globally. That has a nice ring to it, but achieving their goal meant rethinking the whole way that the big corporations, the elephants, work. No longer could the centre dictate it all, as it used to do way back.

Early in my career with Shell, I was responsible for marketing their products in Sarawak in Borneo. It was, in those days, a land of rivers and very few roads. The petrol was used in boats for their outboard motors, not in cars. The manuals for petrol station operation, the rules for their design, the promotional material and reporting forms were all designed in London by people who could not conceive of life, or petrol stations, in a world of rivers. I had to make my own designs and hope that no one would come to check. The experience did at least encourage me to use my initiative but it also provided an early lesson in the futility of trying to run the world from London.

It was also clear, back then, that any attempts by the big organizations to do everything themselves was becoming too expensive and too complicated. Once again, the centre was learning the need to relinquish some operational control. Companies called it out-sourcing or downsizing, and relished the cost-savings that followed. But I was promoting something rather different, what I called the Shamrock Organization – an organization with three integrated leaves made up of the central core, the contractual fringe and the ancillary workforce, a concept that I argued was the way to incorporate a necessary flexibility within a corporate whole. A shamrock, I pointed out, was three leaves that still remained one leaf, which was why St Patrick used it to describe the Christian doctrine of the Trinity – three Gods in one God. I worried that in their haste to dismember the organization and save money, managers were throwing away the sense of belonging that the old companies fostered, and that they would come to regret it. That worry still niggles today.

Nowadays the idea that any corporation can do anything on its own would seem expensive arrogance. Partnership and alliances are in, airlines code-share, automobile companies pool their purchasing, elephants marry their competitor elephants in order to boost their clout or their research budgets, all facilitated by the Internet and the web. Exciting stuff if you are in that world, but the new changes only lend more urgency to the old questions – how do you manage something that you don't fully control? Or trust people whom you never meet? Or belong to something that is more like a bundle of contracts than an extended family with a home?

What is the world of work going to look like in the e-age, with its new mixture of fleas and elephants, with many more fleas, I believe, and fewer but even grander elephants? What is the future of capitalism and how will it change given that value is now vested in knowledge and know-how rather than land and things that you can see and count? How will we manage the new, ever-expanding corporations, and to whom will they be accountable, given that many of them generate more revenue than most countries? How will society adapt to a more virtual world where territorial boundaries are eroded by the Internet? How will taxes be collected? Will the nation state survive or will societies, like corporations, get both bigger and smaller?

Just as the signs were there twenty years ago for those who wished to see them, so I believe we can glimpse the shape of the new capitalist world even if it may take another twenty years to develop. We may not like what is coming but we would be foolish to think that we can plan our lives, or our children's lives, without giving some thought to the shape of the stage on which we and they will be strutting.

Our son is an actor. He spent three long years at drama school learning how to, literally, strut upon a stage and project to an audience. After he graduated it soon became rather obvious that, even though his first love was for the traditional stage, he would need to do quite a lot of film and television work if he wanted to eat. This calls for different skills from those of the stage, yet at no time was any serious attention given in his drama school to developing them. It is absurdly impractical to prepare oneself for the world as it was or as you would like it to be, when the reality is so different, and it is arguably immoral to educate others for a life that can't be lived as it used to be, in a drama school or anywhere else.

My own education was also a relic of the past and absurdly inappropriate for the life that I was going to lead as a flea. Later in the book I examine in more detail what that life involves. There is, I am convinced, no real alternative for most of us. We shall have to live at least some time as a flea, as an independent actor in life. In fact, since the wealth of organizations will be vested in individuals and what they carry in their heads, even the elephants may come to be seen as communities of individual fleas – a healthy change from seeing organizations as collections of human resources, owned by the shareholders.

There is a lot of myself in this book. It is, in parts, an autobiography. Autobiographies can sometimes be self-indulgent hobbies, best reserved for the grandchildren to read after one's death. I could, however, find no better way to illustrate the change from the world of the large organization to the life of an independent than by reviewing my own experience. That transition from elephant inhabitant to independent flea is the transition that many will be required to make in the years to come. For some it will be sooner rather than later. Many will choose to live all their lives as fleas, valuing the freedom of independence over the dubious security of employment. My hope is that my experience of that life will help to make their experience more comfortable, their future more exciting and life more worthwhile.

How do fleas cohabit, for instance? In my organizational world I used to go out to work every day, coming home late in the evening if I wasn't travelling. My wife Elizabeth and I lived separate daytime lives. Our shared interests were our children, our parents and our leisure time, what there was of it. She was always independent, amazed that I would want to sell my precious time to an organization, but how would we arrange our lives when the children grew up and I, too, became a self-employed independent with no workaday home to run to? The research that I had done years earlier on marriage patterns among executives provided some clues, but we found that we had to alter our whole way of life to make the most of our new situation.

How do fleas learn? I have often said that I remembered only one thing from my schooldays, the implicit message that all problems in the world had already been solved, that the answers were to be found in the head of the teacher or, more likely, at the back of his textbook; my task being to transfer those answers to my head. When I joined my corporation I assumed that it was the same: my superiors, or some consultant, would know the answer. It was a shock to realize that I was supposed to come up with my own solutions and that many problems were to do with relationships, where there was no textbook answer. It is better now in most schools, but not much, and I have thoughts for the way it needs to change. But learning does not finish with our schooldays. We should be grateful, because later learning is much more fun.

I have learnt more from art galleries, theatres, cinemas and concert halls than I ever did from textbooks. Travel too, the chance to dwell for a time in other cultures, provides a different lens through which to view one's own world, to question things whose very familiarity have rendered them almost invisible to us. America, India and Italy, three very different cultures, have each taught me a lot. 'Life is for lunch' they say in Tuscany, but they still manage to work productively as well as live convivially, combining leisure and work in a way that eludes other cultures. America, that land of the free, taught me that the future is something to be welcomed because it can be shaped by us, while India's Kerala state demonstrated to me how a combination of socialism and capitalism, properly directed, can transform poverty into prosperity.

Most important of all, however, was the lesson that I learnt from the study of people who create something in their lives out of nothing – we termed them alchemists – for a book that Elizabeth and I undertook between 1997 and 1999. They proved to me that you can learn anything if you really want to. Passion was what drove these people, passion for their product or their cause. If you care enough you will find out what you need to know and chase the source of the knowledge or the skill. Or you will experiment and not worry if the experiment goes wrong. The alchemists never spoke of failures or mistakes but only of learning experiences. Passion as the secret of learning is an odd solution to propose, but I believe that it works at all levels and all ages. Sadly, passion is not a word often heard in the elephant organizations, nor in schools, where it can seem disruptive.

The freedom to control one's own time is one of the great blessings of independence. Accustomed to having to adjust my holiday breaks to the requirements of the organization and the needs of my colleagues, it was a great pleasure to be able to cross out days from the diary without consulting anyone except my wife. The organization of one's time does, however, require the setting of priorities, the making of choices and learning to say 'No'. That in turn demands that you define what success means, something that you can't do without surfacing your true values and beliefs about life and the purpose of life. Something that starts out as a choice between two engagements ends up as a quasi-religious quest.

One of the benefits of life in a large organization had been that that quest could be left aside. Money, status and identity came with the job. By selling time to the corporation one was implicitly accepting their definition of success, at least for that portion of one's life, a portion that, for many of us, has grown larger of recent years. The problem comes later when you have to define yourself without the corporate prop. We had many friends when we lived and worked in Windsor Castle and many invitations to glamorous social events, invitations that mysteriously evaporated after we left. It seemed that for many people we had ceased to exist.

'What will you call yourself when you are independent?' a friend asked me. 'You can't call yourself "past-Warden" for too long.'

'I shall just be Charles Handy,' I said.

'That's brave,' she commented, not very convincingly, and indeed it took me some time to be proud of the fact that at conferences and the like I had no institutional affiliation attached to my name. It felt naked. My wife could not understand my problem. She had never had a job title, nor felt the need for one. Women, I often think, grow up sooner than men, but maybe without the protection of the elephants men too will grow into themselves rather earlier.

We all have skills of some sort. The tricky thing is to turn those skills into a service or a product that people will pay good money for; money may not be the point of life, but it is pretty miserable without it. Actors have their special skills, and their life is a succession of short-term engagements with interludes of what is euphemistically called 'resting' or which our son more practically regards as time for research and self-development. I believe that for many of us life will be very similar.

Actors have agents, however, to promote them, negotiate their contracts and deal with the business sides of their careers so that they can concentrate on the exercise of their professional skills. Fleas need agents too, although they may be called by other names, such as employment agencies, interim management companies or even mutual trade unions. I am lucky, I have publishers whose interest it is to turn me into a brand of sorts, and I have a wife who acts as my agent and managing partner. I notice, in fact, that most of the electricians, plumbers and other independent craftspeople that we employ from time to time also have a partner who acts as the business manager.

This book will dwell on all these issues. It is, if I am honest, a mixture of memories and prejudices, although I would prefer to call them ideas and beliefs. They are the lessons of my life, because I think that you only truly learn by living – and then reflecting on the living. It doesn't mean that all the lessons are correct, of course, but taken together they have become my credo, my way of looking at the different worlds that I have mixed with, my hopes and fears for our futures, and my philosophy for life.

I am conscious, however, that in trying to draw lessons from my own life I am inviting comments such as 'it was easy for you' or 'would that we were all so lucky' or 'it's all very well for some, but not for most of us'. It has not felt easy, and still doesn't, but of course I did start with what some would call the advantage of a privileged education and, most crucially, I married an unusual woman whose fierce belief that we can and should shape our own lives gave me the courage to be a flea when I could easily have settled for a quiet career and early retirement and, no doubt, an early death after a boring life. Most people, anyway, would not envy me my current life of writing and speaking. It can be both lonely and frightening. Don't take my example literally, therefore, but regard this book as an encouragement to write your own script for a part in the very different world that lies ahead of us.

2

BACK TO THE
BEGINNING

It would be pleasing to think that the future was a blank screen on which we could design our future. The reality, as Ernest Hemingway once said, is that the seeds of our life are there from the beginning – if we bother to look. In using my own life as a case study I needed to start by recognizing that 'the past is prologue', as Shakespeare put it.

There is a large oil painting that hangs in the living room of our cottage in the country. Visitors pause by it, puzzled. Why am I dressed as a Victorian cleric? It isn't me, however, just my great-grandfather, Archdeacon of Dublin at the end of the nineteenth century. Our son looks at it in dismay. Is he inevitably going to look like that too? I reassure him. It is my mother's ancestor, not my father's. My wife's family, he knows, are good-looking, English and, unlike mine, keep their hair.

The portrait is a continual reminder, nevertheless, that you are partly the product of your genes. There are some things you can't change. My male ancestors, on both sides, were mostly preachers, going way back. My great-aunts were all teachers. Preachers and teachers; that should have told me something.

Life's other beginnings matter too, the early environment and those first years. I didn't always think so. Or at least I hoped that they didn't, because for a time in my youth I wanted to escape from mine. They defined me too closely. Now I know better. Beginnings always matter. We can fight them, build on them or just accept them, but we can't ignore them or pretend that our lives began later than they really did. Our past is inevitably part of our present and also of our future. I have discovered rather late in life that I needed to be true to myself if I was going to work by myself, to be a flea. It was no use pretending to be someone or something else. Fine, but who was I?

When the stress of my job took me to a psychotherapist he would not talk about my problems until I had told him about my beginnings. 'My early years are not relevant to what I want to talk about,' I told him, irritated. I was in a hurry and I wanted his help to sort out my doubts about the life and new job I was struggling with. I didn't need to tell him the story of my past. But of course those beginnings were horribly relevant, as he eventually helped me to see.

Little things at first. I grew up in St Michael's Vicarage, Sallins, Co. Kildare, where my father was the rector of two small country parishes in the flat lands west of Dublin. He went there when I was two and remained there for forty years. That was the only world I knew in the beginning. The vicarage was our home but also his office, the place where people came to see him. It was my first, although unwitting, school of life.

When the doorbell rang we must always open it, I learnt; it was probably someone needing help. Everyone, I came to understand, had some redeeming features, everyone must be respected, everyone helped, no one turned away or cast aside. Good stuff, and I still believe it, but it was one reason, the psychotherapist suggested, why I was finding it impossible to get rid of some incompetent staff I had inherited in that new job or even to get them to face up to their inadequacies for their work. All my instincts urged me to listen to their woes, to comfort and encourage them when, as their manager, I needed not to comfort but to challenge, to remember the demands of the organization and its clients as well as the needs of the individual in front of me. Even today I find it hard, wrong even, to say no to a request. If someone needs us, I feel, what right do we have to refuse? Which is why we now have a rule that my wife always answers the telephone.

That we must tell the truth, always, no matter how inconvenient, was another lesson from the vicarage. God or his angels will spot the lie, I was told, even if we can conceal it from mere mortals. We will never get away with deceit. I learnt that first the hard way. I must have been about five. We were on holiday in our great-uncle's rectory by the sea and I had taken a cake from the kitchen and eaten it with secret glee in my bedroom. I hoped that they might think that the cat had got it, and denied all knowledge. My mother suspected, confronted me and I confessed. She lectured me, told me to pray for forgiveness, to say sorry to my great-aunt for lying to her and to go to bed without supper. I cried myself to sleep that night, convinced that my life was ruined, all for the sake of a wretched cake. How odd though, I remember thinking, that it wasn't the loss of the cake that upset them all, but my lying about it. It was a lesson that people from John Profumo to Bill Clinton had yet to learn. Lies aren't worth it, I told myself. They boomerang on you.

To this day I am a hopeless negotiator and bargainer, I cannot walk through customs with undeclared goods without being stopped, I cannot say that things are looking up when I know they are heading down, or rally people to a cause that I fear may be lost. Worst of all for the business of life, I assume that other people are like me and are telling the truth at all times, even though hard experience tells me that they are often lying to my face and smiling while they do it. I believe that all alleged criminals who protest their innocence are telling it as it is, until they admit their guilt. It is no good putting me on a jury. This respect for truth can be a big disadvantage, I found. As a manager I accept all promises and undertakings as genuine and I feel very let down when people turn out to be playing me along.

'But surely you didn't believe me, did you?' one property developer asked me in amazement when I accused him of going back on his word. He shook his head, sadly, amazed at my innocence, when I told him that I had never doubted him.

It is difficult when such obvious virtues as a respect for every individual whatever their failings, and for truth whatever the cost, turn out to be disadvantages. It took me many years to come to terms with these consequences of my beginnings and to accept that if I could not change them, did not particularly want to change them, then I had better find a way of life and a part of life where they were not such drawbacks. So it was that I became a flea, with less responsibility for organizing others, and a writer who was free to tell the truth as he saw it.

There were other things, too, hidden in those beginnings, things that I needed to take on board if I was to understand myself. My parents believed that marriage was for life, whatever the difficulties. Nowadays I can see good reasons why people divorce or do not see the point in getting married in the first place. Victorian marriages lasted only fifteen years on average – till death did them part – so perhaps our expectations of relationships that last any longer than those of our forebears are unrealistic. Unhappy marriages may well be worse for everyone concerned than civilized separations.

Nevertheless I couldn't do it. Divorce just wasn't on my parents' agenda, nor is it on ours. Taking it off the agenda for ever alters one's perspectives, I think. It means that when our lives change we can't look for new partners but for new forms of partnership between ourselves, something that became crucially important when I became independent. I notice, however, that the children of divorced parents seem much more likely to end their own marriages in divorce, perhaps because it was very obviously on the agenda in their beginnings.

We didn't hug or kiss or cry much in the vicarage. Emotions were things to be kept under control. I never saw my parents embrace. If my father was upset or angry he would retire to his study, sulk and simmer on his own until he felt better. I do the same; bottling it up, my wife calls it. It was thought selfish, maybe, to impose your emotions on others in case they did not want them. Even today my sisters and I do not kiss or even rub cheeks when we meet. I regret this aspect of my beginnings, I must say, and I rejoice that it is one thing that has not been passed on to our own children.

It can't be a total accident, either, that today our home is also my office, as the vicarage was for my father, that people come to see us there, that it is where we hold our meetings, and where I, like him, do my reading and my writing, although not the prayers, at least not the sort of praying that we did back then. Every morning at 8.30 he would walk the two hundred yards up the road to say matins, alone in his church. The dogs would go with him but wait outside. It was his private quiet time at the start of the day. That wasn't the end of the praying, however. There would then be the family prayers, *de rigueur* for all of us, no lying-in at the vicarage. They happened around the breakfast table before we ate, kneeling at our chairs. My father would rattle through the prayers for the day while the dogs licked our faces, the toast burned and the telephone rang. In my secular agnostic teens I cringed when my friends from school or college came to stay. I would pretend that breakfast started fifteen minutes later so that they would miss the prayers, only to find that they relished this throwback to better days and the experience of a family praying together.

That tradition has long passed for me now, but traces remain. I take a walk every morning before breakfast, without dogs but with Elizabeth. Days without an early walk don't seem to start right. It's a form of perambulating meditation, getting oneself straight before work begins. And I can't stay in bed beyond nine o'clock. It would feel wrong, as if I was missing something that I shouldn't. Those who start the day together, stay together, I like to think.

Those were some of the traditions that stuck. Other parts of our beginnings can, however, trigger an opposite reaction, a determination to do it differently, to buck the tradition. We were not rich. My father had a stipend, not a salary. The difference is that a salary is supposed to be a reflection of your worth as measured by the market for your type of skills and talents, while a stipend is the provision of just enough money to enable you to do your job. Our house was provided by the parish but not its furnishings or its lighting and heating. The small stipend was supposed to pay for those plus our food and clothing. You did not become a priest to make more money than was needed. I can't say that we suffered in any way, but I grew up knowing that money was precious and must only be spent on things that lasted, not on ephemeral things like eating out, going to the theatre or on holiday trips; these were rare treats for special occasions.

I hankered, therefore, for a life where money could be wasted on ephemera. I still relish the chance to throw money at a restaurant meal, a luxury hotel or a good bottle of wine – things that at best leave only memories. I like renting or hiring, not buying; it leaves more cash to spend in the short term. Fortunately for our financial ease I married a woman who was reacting the other way against a rather profligate father. She regards money spent on things that leave only memories as money wasted. An investment, on the other hand, she sees as money stored for the future. Our life is a precarious balance, therefore, between my desire for profligacy and hers for prudence; both of them because of revolt against our beginnings.

Maybe it was an early reaction to our obvious lack of spending money that caused me to do something that still puzzles and shames me. When I was seven or eight I started to pick up, steal actually, odd coins that I would find lying around the house, loose change from my mother's shopping or, more shameful still, the odd coins from my grandmother's purse when she came to stay (she was too old and doddery to notice, I was sure). I didn't do anything with these coins, I just hoarded them in a drawer in my room. They weren't for spending, as I recall, just for looking at. It was a mild form of kleptomania, maybe, or an incipient love of money for its own sake, the kind of thing that I would later find writ large in America. I went off to a boarding school when I was nine, and a few weeks later I got a letter from my mother. 'I found a pile of coins in a drawer in your room,' she wrote. 'I can't think how they got there so I put them in the collecting box for the Mission to Lepers.' The subject was never mentioned again.

I wonder now whether I was not subconsciously imitating my father. He was a hoarder, a careful custodian of money, both his own and other people's. He followed Polonius's advice to 'neither a borrower nor a lender be'. His uncle sold a small farm near Londonderry in 1946 for £14,000, a reasonable sum at the time. A man without family of his own, he left the money in trust for me, with the income going to himself and then my father for as long as they lived. Two years before he died, my father needed it to buy a house for his retirement. He showed me the accounts for the trust, proud that they still showed a sum of £14,000. I was tempted to remark that he had misunderstood the parable of the talents, but that would have been tactless. He was not a speculator.

Neither am I. I went to business school; I know that the way to get rich is to make money at a higher rate than it costs you. Borrowing is called gearing, a way to get up speed. Instinctively, however, I prefer to accumulate the money first, then spend it, rather than to borrow and pay it back, just like my father who, I often thought, regarded an overdraft as a sin only marginally above adultery. Which is why, I ruefully acknowledge, I would never be a successful entrepreneur or get rich. How, I wonder now, did I ever think that I could be a businessman?

There's another lesson from my drawer of secret coins, I reflected years later: money hoarded, doing nothing and not needed, is money wasted. Give it away or it will be taken from you, somehow. It's a lesson that the great philanthropists of America, Carnegie, Rockefeller and others, learnt and practised to the good of their society. It is one of my great hopes for the future that private philanthropy will ultimately redeem some of the extremes of capitalism, allowing those who have collected far more coins than they could conceivably need to give them away before they are taken from them.

We went to church, every Sunday, every major feast day and every carol service. It was an unusual church for the Irish countryside, all marble inside with romanesque arches and intricate mosaics, inspired by an Italian church that had impressed its benefactor, who had provided the money for it a hundred years before. I loved the building but reacted against the doctrine and dogma it stood for. The idea that the Son of God was following me around, standing beside me or over me, ready to help or criticize, felt bizarre and claustrophobic. I know now that this was a travesty of Christianity but that was how it felt at the time. In my teens I swore a private oath that when I was free I would not be poor again or go to church again, ever. Yet thirty years later I found myself living on a clergy salary and going to church, not just on Sundays, but every day. Life has a way of rewinding itself. You just hope that it is doing so in a spiral, going upwards.

What did stick from all that churchgoing in my youth was the language. Jeremy Paxman has an interesting section on the Church of England in his fascinating book *The English*. The dissolution of the monasteries in 1536 not only stripped the Roman Catholic Church of its earthly powers, he says, it was also an enormous act of collective vandalism which involved the smashing of thousands of pieces of art. In so doing an entire medieval tradition of painting and sculpture which survived elsewhere in Europe was, in England, wiped from the slate. In its place, however, came a new literary tradition heralded by William Tyndale's first Bible in English and Cranmer's prayer book. The Authorized Version of the Bible arrived in 1611 and the Book of Common Prayer in 1662. These two 'reservoirs of language' gave the English, says Paxman, a love of words.

They did the same for me. Sunday after Sunday, morning prayers after morning prayers, the sonorous phrases and beautiful cadences wormed their way into my memory. My father spoke them beautifully. I still treasure the sheer verbal thrill of Sunday morning communion services with him presiding, albeit feeling guilty as I said the words but denied their meaning. 'May the Lord prevent us in all our doings,' I would pray, thinking 'That's just typical of religion, asking God to stop everything I want to do,' unaware at the time that in 1662 'prevent' meant 'go before'.

Years later, when I showed my mother something that I had written, she commented adversely on my use of jargon. 'I would have thought that you could have found the words to describe anything you want to say somewhere in the Book of Common Prayer or the works of Shakespeare.' Indeed, and the rhythms too. I have tried to remember her advice ever since. I can see why the Churches want to rewrite their liturgies and bring the translations of the Bible up to date, but I am happy that I got the earlier versions. They helped to make me what I am today, a wordsmith. A reviewer said of my first book, a textbook, that there was nothing in it that had not been said before – the difference was that much of it had not been read before. I liked that.

Shakespeare was another sort of bible, just as misunderstood by me in my early years but equally a part of life and a source of verbal magic. It was enough to roll the lines around my tongue, never mind what they meant or to whom they were delivered. I occasionally spent part of my holidays with my cousins and a bevy of maiden aunts and great-aunts. Ireland, the middle-class Protestant Ireland of the south was then full of unmarried women of two generations, for the men they might have married had been killed in the two world wars. At one time I counted fourteen unmarried great-aunts. There was no television then, so of an evening we might read a Shakespeare play aloud together, appropriately bowdlerized by Great-Aunt Augusta. I suspect that I enjoy it more now in retrospect than I did at the time, but the language resonated then, and does now.

All those aunts! I grew up in the company of women, two younger sisters, no brothers, no boys nearby. My father was a quiet man, sports were not his thing, except for a bit of trout fishing in August on holiday. I never learnt to sail, ski, play football, shoot or hunt or fish. Such things are best learnt young and easiest to learn if they form part of the pattern of the life around you. Horses there were in abundance in that part of Ireland, and for a time I had my own pony, Mavourneen, but I was no good at managing the beast, did not enjoy it, was shamed by my younger sisters' prowess and soon gave it up. I later learnt to play golf and tennis badly and rugby football even worse, but I have always regretted that my beginnings were not more physically active.

The trouble is that the sins and omissions of the fathers do get passed on to the children, 'even unto the third and fourth generations'. Because I didn't do these things our children, in turn, missed out. Our beginnings are the responsibility of our parents, but parents mostly have not lived long enough at the time to have understood how their own beginnings have shaped their ends. Maybe that's for the best. There is, after all, no way of predicting how your children will react to the beginnings you may shape for them. Try too hard to condition your young and you may only stoke rebellion. Nevertheless the atmosphere we parents create, the values we live by, the priorities that we allocate, these make up the only world the young child knows. Home is the first school for us all, a school with no fixed curriculum, no quality control, no examinations and no teacher training. No wonder my first thought as I watched our daughter being born was, 'What have I taken on?' Too late!

Until recently, I had not revisited my childhood for many years. Maybe I was trying to forget it. As I retraced my steps for this book I began to wonder whether things really did happen as I recalled. We all mythologize our personal histories, but, as Gabriel García Márquez, that magical storyteller, says in the introduction to his own autobiography, 'what matters in life is not what happens to you, but what you remember and how you remember it.'

Whatever the truth of my beginnings I wanted to leave them. I needed to get rich and keep out of churches. It took a shock to recall me to my hidden roots. In 1981 I was asked by BBC television to contribute to a series they were running on Sunday evenings called *The Light of Experience*. They would ask someone who had gone through a critical experience to talk about it straight to camera, reading off an autocue a script that they had written themselves, interleaved with photographs from their private album. There was a woman who had been in a Thai gaol for drug smuggling, a barrister who had married the murderer she defended in court, others who had been through unusual crises or events that had changed their lives.

My experience was different, I told the BBC. It was very usual, even universal. It was the death of my father. It will be good, they said, to have something more ordinary, if you are prepared to say why it wasn't ordinary for you. Rashly, perhaps, I agreed. I have spoken and written of his death elsewhere, but this is the heart of what I said then.

My father was a quiet man. He had been rector of the same parish in Kildare in southern Ireland for forty years when he retired, aged seventy-two. He was tired by then, understandably. For the last fourteen of those years he had also been archdeacon of the diocese. He died two years later.

I was in Paris at a business conference when I heard that he was dying. I flew back to Dublin, but he was unconscious by the time I got there and died the next day. His funeral, like all funerals in Ireland, was arranged for the day after tomorrow, a quiet family affair, back in the country church he served for so long.

I was very fond of my father, but disappointed in him. He had turned down big city parishes, had settled for a humdrum life in the same little backwater. His life seemed to be a series of boring meetings and visits punctuated with the unchanging rhythm of Sundays with old Mrs Atkinson and Eddie to lunch in the vicarage afterwards. I would, I determined, lead a different life.

At the time he died I was a professor at the new London Business School, gallivanting around to conferences, consulting, lunching, dining, on the edge of the big time. A book had been published, and articles galore. We had two young children, a flat in town, and a cottage in the country. More than that, I was tremendously busy, with a diary crammed with engagements. Success!

With these thoughts in mind I followed the hearse down the country roads to my father's funeral; a quiet end for a quiet man, I reflected. A pity that he had never really understood what I was doing. When I became a professor my mother's reaction had been to ask whether it meant that I could now spend more time with the children.

Suddenly I noticed that we seemed to have a police escort; the local police had decided, unasked, to clear a route for the last few miles to the church. A nice compliment to a Protestant vicar in rural Catholic Ireland but just as well, because it was hard to thread our way between the queues of cars trying to get to the little country church. The place was packed, overflowing. How had they heard? He had only died the day before yesterday, and there had been just the one notice in one paper.

The choir looked odd, too. Dressed in the little-boy surplices that I remembered from Sundays long ago, but with older faces. I remembered some of them. Choir boys and choir girls reassembled from all corners of Ireland, and from England too. They had dropped everything to be there. The Archbishop, supposed to be in hospital and still propped on a stick, was there to say to all of us how special my father had been, how he would be missed but remembered for ever by so many whose lives he had touched.

As I stood by his grave, surrounded by the people he had helped to marry, whose children he had baptized and then seen marry in his church in their turn, as I saw the tears in the eyes of the hundreds of people who had come from everywhere to say farewell to this 'quiet' man, I turned away and began to think.

Who, I wondered, would come to my funeral with tears in their eyes? What is success and who was the successful one, me or my father? What is one's life for, and what is the point of our existence in this world? They are not exactly new questions. I had studied philosophy. I knew the theories. I had never applied them to myself before. Not seriously.

I went back to England. It was a long hot summer that year. I resolved to change my life and my priorities. I thought that I might go to theological college, might become ordained as a priest like my father. Luckily, I now think, the bishops whom I approached told me not to be so silly. If I wanted to serve God, as they put it, I could do it much better as a professor of business than in a dog collar.

They encouraged me to apply for the post of Warden of St George's House in Windsor Castle. This small select study centre was established by Prince Philip and the then Dean of Windsor, Robin Woods, to be a meeting place for people of influence in the churches and in other parts of society. It ran consultations on topics like justice, the future of work, power and responsibility in society – consultations at which captains of industry, trade union leaders, head teachers, civil servants and politicians mingled and debated with bishops and chaplains and each other. It was a place of retreat and reflection for busy people in a busy world, set in a courtyard behind St George's Chapel. It was to be my home and my workplace for the next four years.

My beginnings had finally caught up with me. T.S. Eliot said, 'to return to the place where you started, and know it now for the first time'; that was me. But my new job in Windsor was not easy. I was, I discovered, very much a man under authority and I remembered what an earlier boss had once told me about my inability to work under others. Nor was I the strong and forceful manager that the place needed. I was unhappy and stressed, the things that took me to the psychotherapist in the first place. I discovered only then that I needed him to explain to me that my problems might be because I had not fully understood what sort of person I was. 'Know Yourself' was the maxim of the ancient Greeks, inscribed over the temple of Apollo at Delphi. I now believe that is difficult to do until you have gone through the process of knowing who you are not. That takes time, but in my mid-forties I was nearly there, having crossed several roles and careers off my list.

Elizabeth, my wife, knows me better than I know myself. 'It's time for you to get out of organizations,' she said, after four years in that castle in Windsor.

'But what will I do?' I asked. 'How will we earn money?'

'You like writing, don't you, and your first book seems to be a success, so why not be a writer?'

'You don't get rich writing books,' I complained.

'Why do you want to be rich? We can survive. I can work as well as you, and you can probably do some occasional teaching on management courses if you need to.'

'It's risky.'

'It's life. And I'm tired of living with a stressed-out zombie.'

So began my life as an independent, as a flea.

For the next few years I carried around a small card in my pocket. It had two columns on it, 'In' and 'Out' for my guesses at income and expenditure for the year ahead. The 'Out' column always seemed the bigger at the beginning of the year but the 'In' usually made it up by the end. I should have been worried, but I wasn't. It was such a relief not having to look over my shoulder for approval, to be fully in charge of my own life for the first time, not to have to pretend to be anything that I wasn't, to know myself at last and to be comfortable in my own skin.

Some get there quicker than I did. Some never do, perhaps don't want to.

There were things that I missed, naturally, when I left the world of organizations. I missed the comfort of belonging to something bigger than myself, the feeling that even if you were ill or absent the world would go on. As an independent, if you don't make it happen it won't happen. That keeps you on your toes, but sometimes it would be nice to sit back on your heels and let others take the strain. I missed the supporting infrastructure. In Shell it was massive. They even filled in my tax returns for me. In Windsor the help was minimal, but there was still someone who did the accounts, someone who kept the records and the files, a secretary who kept my diary and helped to ease my life. Now I had to do all these things myself.

Most of all, I missed my colleagues. Not that I always agreed with them, or even liked them all particularly, but they were people to share problems with, people whose concerns for the work gelled with mine, people who formed a community, whose lives were partly interwoven with mine, people to gossip with, brainstorm with, bitch about the world with, companions for a while on life's journey.

We all need somewhere to belong. There is a loneliness in going it alone that is the other side of freedom. How I struggled to deal with these dilemmas is the subject of another chapter.

Weighed in the scales of happiness, however, there is no doubt; freedom wins every time.

I write this book, however, because I believe that the world we are entering is increasingly the world of the individual, of choice and of risk. It won't always be a comfortable world and the risks are high, but there is now more chance than ever to shape our own lives, to be fully ourselves. Life is longer now. We can live at least three lives in one lifetime, and one of them will, I am sure, have to be the life of a flea. I have found that to be the best of my different lives.

But that all came later. First I had to go to school, to be schooled for what everyone assumed would be life in some sort of organization. That was the way it was then.

3

SCHOOLS FOR AN OLD WORLD

Whoever it was who said that your schooldays were the happiest days of your life must have been either a masochist or had a very bad memory, I reflected as I left my last school on my last day. I hoped fervently that it wasn't true, otherwise I was going to have a very sad life.

I left persuaded that the world thus far was unfair, punitive and unpleasant. The best way to survive was to find out what the rules were, to keep your head down and pass the tests that the authorities set you as best you could. It was not the best way to prepare for the independent life, but that was the last thing I was thinking of. I was going to another institution, a university, which would, I trusted, provide me with the credentials for further institutions, where I would endeavour to keep the rules and pass their tests until death or retirement overtook me.

That was my reaction to a succession of coercive establishments. Others with different personalities might have reacted differently. My wife went to eleven, mostly incompetent, schools before she was sixteen. She came away believing that rules were there to be challenged, that those in authority often got it wrong, and that you had to stand up for yourself in this world, because no one else might. But she was destined to be a flea from her beginnings.

I left school certain of one thing, that I wasn't going to end up as a teacher. But of course, that is exactly what happened, although in a way I could not have anticipated. Ten years later I was educating managers for Shell, and my life thereafter has been involved in education in one way or another. I have been determined that it should be done differently and better than the ways that I had experienced. I haven't always succeeded, but my experiences were the starting point for the views that I developed and that I still believe to be relevant and important, even though schools are much changed from the ones that I knew.

There were no pre-school play groups or kindergartens in rural Ireland. I had governesses instead, first Phoebe, then Joan – or was it the other way round? I have no idea how my parents could have afforded it. I can only suppose that these young women did it for food and board and a bit of pocket money, rather like au pairs today. I have only warm fuzzy memories of those years. Was it they who taught me to read and write and count? I imagine so, because I could do these things moderately well when I went to my first proper school, the local primary or 'national' school, half a mile down the road, at the age of six.

It was freezing cold in that schoolroom, that I do remember, with only one coal-fired stove to keep us warm. Chilblains, a word my children do not know, made my fingers swell up, turning itchy and raw. It cannot help towards a love of learning that schools so often can be such uncomfortable places, apparently designed to mortify the flesh. We sat on hard wooden benches while we were drilled on our multiplication tables, recited bits and pieces of poems or psalms that we had been told to memorize as our homework, and mouthed parrot-fashion a few phrases of the compulsory Irish language. What it was all about or for, I had no idea. It was just what one did as a child, it seemed, a form of purgatory before one reached the heaven of being grown up. It helped a little that I was quite good at these tricks. It meant that the smacks on my open palm with a hard wooden ruler didn't happen too often.

I learnt there that what you learn through fear seldom sticks. I wanted to forget the lessons along with the memories of the unpleasantness. We learn best and most when we want to learn. I suspect that the Harry Potter books and teletext messages on mobile phones have done more to encourage the young to read than any number of literacy hours.

If the schoolroom was unpleasant, the playground was worse. I had grown up thus far in the company of women. In addition to my mother and the governesses I had two younger sisters, but in that remote Irish countryside I knew no other boys until I went to school. Unusually for a primary school it also boarded some twenty boys, who had no local school of their own. They were the insiders, of course, the resident gang, while I was the shy outsider. I was teased rather than bullied and I fear that I never did learn to fight back. Instead I tried to court popularity, wanting desperately to be liked, to be included. I suspect that I demeaned myself, flattered the big boys unnecessarily and insincerely, aped their ways and longed to be part of their clubs; because that is what I have been tempted to do throughout most of my life ever since.

Was I born like that, I wonder now, or did those early days of schooling scar me for life? And did Mr Crawford, the benign but rather remote master in charge, realize that what went on in that concrete playground was having more impact on me, and presumably on all the others, than the lessons in the schoolroom? School is, for most of us, the first experience that we have of a society wider than our own family, our first taste of formal authority, of hierarchies both formal and informal, of peer groups and gangs, of dealing with people to whom we aren't related, who don't know us and may not want us around. It needs, as far as we can engineer it, to be a positive experience. Yes, of course we should learn to read and write and count at an early stage because these few basic skills are the entry gates to the rest of life, but it's no good being able to open those gates if you can't cope with the human systems behind them. Would-be fleas, in particular, need to leave their first schools with their self-confidence intact. I didn't.

I was not sad to be leaving that place at the age of nine, although I was going to another medieval institution – a boys' preparatory school, far from home, where I would be a boarder, getting home only for the holidays. I remember, as must others who have gone to these places, the sight of my parents walking away, while I was whisked upstairs by the headmaster's wife to my new world, trying to hide my tears. Strange and lonely though it was at first, it was actually an improvement on what had gone before. At least there were others like me, and in a bigger institution there was room to have one's own gang.

That said, the staff common room seemed to be a refuge for sadist misfits. This was one of a few Protestant preparatory schools for the dwindling numbers of the Anglo-Irish gentry. It was wartime, and, although Ireland was officially neutral, most of the able-bodied Anglo-Irish had gone off to join the British army, leaving us with the residue. I was unfortunate enough to be a member of the two top forms when the headmaster decided to beat us all, six strokes with a cane on the bare behind, because a boy in the bottom form had stolen a bar of chocolate. We were responsible, he claimed, for not setting a better example. He had a point, I recognized later in my life; those at the top of organizations do indeed set the culture; but at the time I just thought it grossly unfair.

Beatings were a way of life there, as were the cold baths that we lined up for every morning, naked and shivering, under the stern gaze of the head. It was supposed to toughen us up, but I can't help now suspecting more devious motives. No doubt the place would be closed down these days, but I can't honestly say that it affected us much. We accepted it all as part of the rum world that we were part of, and assumed it was warning us of the arbitrary ways of society outside. Which, in a sense, it probably was. My complaint would be that it wasn't helping us to deal with society's challenges, only to endure them. Keep your mouth shut and stay out of sight were two of the lessons that I carried away with me.

Then something happened that was to influence my life and career ever after. A friend, another Charles, was due to take the scholarship examination for Winchester College. He would have to learn Greek to do so, but the school taught only Latin. A special tutor was arranged for him, an eccentric elderly clergyman from Dublin. Charles asked if I would take the lessons with him, for companionship. I agreed, more for his sake than mine, without thinking about it too much – I was only twelve. I enjoyed these lessons. Our eccentric clergyman taught us Ancient Greek as if it was a normal foreign language, by encouraging us to talk it out loud and to think as Greeks, while all the time introducing us to the myths and history of that civilization. What you enjoy you usually do well. When I, in my turn, had to take an examination for a scholarship it was obvious that I should offer Latin and, particularly, Greek as my subjects. I passed.

And so it was that I became, by chance, a classical scholar of sorts. Under the English system of education whereby you do best by concentrating on your two or three best subjects, I remained defined as a classicist right through to the end of my university years. As a result, I never had a single science lesson, was not allowed to pursue my interest in mathematics because the timetable did not permit such a mix of subjects, and had to abandon other languages at the age of fifteen. I often wonder what would have happened without that invitation to learn Greek.

I discovered later in life that I had been trained as a hedgehog when I was really a fox. Remember the saying of the Greek poet Archilochus as famously told to Isaiah Berlin by Lord Oxford: 'The fox,' said Archilochus, 'knows many things, but the hedgehog knows one big thing.' The English persist in growing hedgehogs when the world needs a mix of both to keep itself flexible as well as expert.

I would not now ask anyone to decide their future at the age of fifteen, let alone at twelve as I did. Life is long. We should keep our options open for as long as possible. An educational system that judges people on their demonstrated proficiency in a subject rather than their potential for future learning is unreasonable. It condemns young people to decide their future on the basis of what subjects they happen to favour in their mid teens, a decision often influenced by what teachers they happen to have encountered along the way, or by what the school timetable allows.

The consequences for the traditional English system of education are considerable if they wish to grow more foxes. Better measures of potential would need to be developed by university recruiters. Undergraduate courses would have to be extended to allow for the specialist study previously done in the final years of school. University teachers would need to teach subjects at a lower level than they have been accustomed to. The sources of likely resistance to any change are clear. Yet every continental European country, as well as the United States, maintains a more open and broader system of education. So does Scotland. England needs to do likewise or she risks imprisoning her young. Why, I wonder, do universities have such an influence on the work of our schools when, even today, only one third of an age group go on to study there? It is perhaps no surprise that many of the alchemists whom my wife and I studied for our book chose to escape from the English system as early as they could. There was too little room for experimentation, too little chance to demonstrate potential as opposed to proficiency.

I discovered something else, by chance, in that preparatory school. I was born in late July. Schools then, as now, classify their students by their age at the beginning of the school year in September. Those born in July or August are either six months older than the average, or six months younger. They, or more often their parents, have the choice of pushing them forward or holding them back. In one's teens those six months can make a difference. In retrospect I was lucky, for I sat my exams late rather than early throughout my schooldays, which in effect gave me an extra year of study. No wonder I did quite well. But I also found myself, in my final year at that early school, a little older than everyone else. So it was that I was appointed head boy for six months.

It was a largely symbolic role. I had the responsibility for keeping order in break times, without any carrots or sticks to enforce it, and to set standards of behaviour generally. I was supposed to do this by force of personality, something that I felt I rather obviously lacked. I don't suppose I did it very well, but I learnt that the role can make the man, that, amazingly, people are willing to accept you at your own valuation. As I grew more sure of myself I was surprised to find that a room of sixty young boys actually stopped talking when I asked them to, even without raising my voice. It did wonders for my self-confidence, all because I stayed on for a year longer than I needed to.

I wonder, as a result, why it is that so many want to accelerate the education of their young. Being a little older than my peers was no cause for shame. I doubt, in fact, that anyone knew it. Yet my extra months gave me extra maturity and extra time for study. I was a year older than some when I went to university, but there were many there who had done what was then their National Service in the armed forces and were at least a year older than me, although it often seemed more. I am sure that they got more out of their university experience than I did. Elizabeth started university in her forties; our daughter was thirty-three when she obtained her degree. Like many of today's mature students they went when they were ready to study, not because it was part of society's hurdle race.

More generally, I now deplore the age fixation that afflicts so much of education. The present British government, with its fondness for league tables and standards of every sort, likes to test children at seven, eleven, fourteen and sixteen, in spite of the fact that everyone agrees that children, like adults, learn at different paces in different subjects. Universal and standard tests at given ages inevitably lead to comparisons across the board. Since we tend to compare ourselves with those above us rather than those below, the results are depressing for most.

What's the great hurry? We don't require everyone in the UK

to pass their driving test at a given age. If we did, and then published the scores in league tables, we would probably fail the bottom half. It might clear up the roads but it would immobilize and effectively disenfranchise a large chunk of the population. That, I believe, is what we risk doing with age-related tests in schools.

Music, oddly, is different. Children take their examinations for their music grades when their teacher thinks they are ready, irrespective of their age. As a result, the examinations are usually an occasion for celebration, and there are no complaints of falling standards.

My traditional British public school was another ordeal. Education, I felt, was becoming a cruel game of snakes and ladders. Just when you had reached the top of one pile you had to start again at the bottom of another. If life was going to go like that, I remember thinking, then I don't think I want it. My new school was an ancient grammar school foundation gone private and aping the worst traditions of its bigger brothers. Those in the bottom two forms were called 'douls' – Greek for slaves, as I knew only too well. Senior monitors, or prefects, had their own douls. They could also give a 'doul call'. When the fancy took them they would yell 'Doul' down the passageways and we luckless ones had to drop everything and run, the last to arrive being handed the job that the monitor wanted doing, usually some completely trivial errand.

The place abounded in rules and rituals, many of them dating from previous centuries with no perceptible rationale. We had to spend the first weeks learning them by heart. Punishment at its most lenient consisted of 'lines' – writing out a hundred or more lines of the wretched rule book – but could mean a beating by the monitors, several of them, each taking turns to run across the changing room to swish a cane across one's bottom. The indignity of that particular ritual was worse than the hurt. I learnt a lot about the irresponsible use of power in my years there. On the other hand, there were also kind and sensible young men who eschewed such practices, who helped to run the houses that made up the school in a constructive way, and who went out of their way to help younger boys.

Shutting four hundred adolescent boys up together for months at a time can't be a sensible idea. Having started my life surrounded by women, I was now immersed in a male hothouse. There was no television at that time, we heard no radio, saw no newspapers, so were entirely obsessed with ourselves. A group of us agreed to write diaries one term. I found mine, by chance, the other day and was horrified to find how trivial my life was, how preoccupied with whether I was in or out of this gang or that. Illicit passions bubbled below the surface. Sex was the great taboo, and sex or anything like it, with anyone of either gender, meant instant expulsion. We weren't supposed to have private conversations with anyone more than one form above or below us – just in case. Unbelievably, our trouser pockets were sewn up until we reached the senior forms aged sixteen, in case we fingered ourselves. Small wonder, I suppose, that I felt repressed and confused.

That was all fifty years ago, and the place has changed beyond all recognition, as it needed to. For one thing it is now co-educational. But the concept of giving some limited responsibilities to older students does seem to have value, as long as there are reasonable constraints on their powers. It is one way of exposing young people to a sense of responsibility for others and of offsetting what is otherwise an emphasis on purely personal achievement, which can easily lead to a careless selfishness. It is one of the traditions of the private schools that was, in my view, wrongly abolished by the state system, probably because of the sort of excesses that I experienced.

In later years I was commissioned to make a study comparing schools to other organizations. I visited many schools of all shapes and sizes. My first, casual, question on arriving in the staff common room would be to ask how many people worked there. Primary schools might say ten, the larger secondary schools seventy or eighty.

'Oh dear,' said a Director of Education when I told him this, 'they left out the cleaners.'

'No,' I replied, 'they left out the children.'

Organizationally, the students weren't seen as members of the organization but more as its products, perhaps more accurately as its work in progress. And that, so often, was the way they were treated, passed from work station to work station, shaped here, polished a bit there, lined up for inspection at the end, the failures rejected but not recycled, the rest publicly graded for future use by someone. My boarding school worked like that.

My knowledge of Latin and Greek helped me in the classroom, but did nothing for my popularity. Sporting prowess was what counted, and I never got beyond the Third XV in rugby and scorer for the cricket team. But I was lucky once again. My form master, who was also my house master, was a great teacher of the classics, and a true educationalist, who saw it as his mission not only to bring out the best in us but to civilize us, by introducing us to the best of music, literature and poetry. He came into class one morning where we waited to analyse another hundred lines of Virgil's *Aeneid*.

'Did any of you recognize the organ voluntary in chapel this morning?' he asked. None of us had even been listening, of course.

'It was one of Bach's greater pieces,' he said. 'Come, it's time you understood what you were missing.' He took us back to his house and spent the rest of the morning playing us Bach's music and introducing us to his story. If it wasn't Bach it was Wilfred Owen or William Blake, or, on one occasion, a wine tasting as a prelude to bottling his imported cask from France. His classes were enlivened and enriched by these unexpected interludes, none of which were in anyone's curriculum but which I now remember long after I have forgotten Virgil's verses.

We called him 'Slaver' because he worked us so hard, but we said it affectionately because he so obviously believed in us and in our potential. It is a vital ingredient in life to receive a 'golden seed' early on from someone you respect, a compliment or an expression of confidence in you that fortifies self-belief. The Slaver gave me mine. It is still, I believe, the greatest gift that a teacher can give a pupil, at any age. I shall always be grateful, although I suspect that my subsequent career as an oil executive must have seemed to him a waste of his efforts. He was all that a great teacher should be, and he, quite deliberately, changed my life, insisting that I should try for an entrance scholarship to Oxford rather than Trinity College, Dublin, where my father had gone and his father before him.

I went up to Oxford for the exam, intending to use it as a practice run, but, as luck would have it, I was granted a major scholarship by Oriel College. The bird in the hand is the safer option, I reflected, so I accepted, not realizing that by so doing I was effectively leaving Ireland, because Oxford would redefine me as sort of English. The Slaver was right, however. The Oxford system of learning, of one-to-one tutoring, of weekly essays and lots of discretionary time, suited me well. It was horribly privileged, I now realize, and the individual tutorial system for undergraduates is too expensive to last, but I'm glad that I was able to experience it. Classics at Oxford started with the language, but moved on to the study of the history of Greece and Rome and the philosophical tradition that they started. I was encouraged to explore ideas and hypotheses, to reach beyond the knowledge and the facts to what they meant. My schooling had finished, my education had begun. I was starting to think for myself at last.

I still felt useless, able only to turn English into Greek or vice versa, but, as time went on, I saw that the subject matter hadn't been all that important – and I have long ago forgotten all of it. What really mattered was the process, the need to work things out for myself for a change. Once, when my social life was overfull, I copied out my essay from a rather obscure book on Greek history and read it to my tutor. He made no comment. In an ominous silence he walked over to his bookcase, took down his copy of that obscure history, found the page and continued to read from the point where I had finished. I blushed in shame. Nothing more needed to be said. Oxford wasn't interested in the repetition of other people's work until and unless it had become part of one's own thinking.

And yes, I read my essay out loud. That was what we used to

do. I put it down then to laziness on the part of the tutors, although I think that it may have required more mental energy to listen than to read. What I do know is that it changed my writing style. I have never been able to write the long parenthetical sentences that academics are so good at. You can't read them out loud. It was, if nothing else, a great training for broadcasting. Later I was told that Italian children are examined orally in most subjects; no wonder Italians are so articulate, so addicted to their phones rather than the Internet.

Our schools, I now think, need a process curriculum as well as a content curriculum. Twenty years ago I was one of a group that started a campaign that we called Education for Capability. We said, in a public manifesto, that a well-balanced education should, of course, embrace analysis and the acquisition of knowledge. But it must also include the exercise of creative skills, the competence to undertake and complete tasks and the ability to cope with everyday life; as well as doing all these things in co-operation with others.

For our campaign I went to address the staff of one of the country's prestigious private schools. The headmaster rose at the end to thank me. 'I sense,' he said, 'that you would disapprove of much of what we do in our classrooms, but you would be surprised by how closely we follow your ideals outside the classroom, in everything that our pupils do, be it on the playing fields, in their drama or music sessions, in their clubs, workshops and community work.'

'I'm sure you are right,' I replied. 'The trouble is that not all schools have the time and the facilities for such learning beyond the classroom and the curriculum.'

If I were in charge of our schools I would be tempted to divide the day in half, one half to be spent in the classroom acquiring knowledge and the skills of analysis, the other half outside, on projects and activities that would cultivate process skills and experiences. We might need a different set of teachers for each, but the process skills could well be taught by volunteers from the community, through apprenticeships or through attachments to ongoing projects.

I left Oxford with a lucky first-class degree. I was overjoyed, and my parents were pleased, but the truth is that no one ever asked me for the class of my degree until I applied to another academic establishment. I wonder why we bother with all our grades and gradations which cause so much heartache, if all that really matters is whether we passed or not. When our son started his acting career he showed me the mini-biography that he had composed to go in the theatre programme. I liked it, I said, but wondered why he hadn't made any mention of his education and his grades, which were something I felt he could be justifiably proud of.

'Dad,' he said, rather condescendingly, 'in the theatre world people aren't interested in where you got educated or what exams you passed. What they want to know is what you have done with it.' Point taken.

I was, however, startled to find that, as a graduate, I was part of a small minority in the Britain of my day. In those years only 8 per cent of an age group went to university and it showed up later. When I was inquiring into systems of management education in the eighties I discovered that nine out of ten of all the people aged over fifty in 1980 had left school at age fifteen and had not had any formal education since. It explained a lot about the lack of visionary leadership at the top of British business in those years, because most of the 10 per cent who did stay on at school went into the professions or into government service, leaving business bereft of widely read or inquiring minds.

The French want 75 per cent of an age group to go on to some sort of further education after school. For that to happen in Britain it has to be made more affordable. Part-time studies, distance learning as in the Open University, and evening courses must become the norm so that people can earn while they learn. The prestige universities will then gradually become graduate schools, supported by research grants and by students who can expect their graduate degrees to repay the cost of their studies.

As for myself, I thought that I had finished with education when I left Oxford and joined the so-called school of life. I regret, now, that I didn't take up the option of two years of National Service in the armed services. By all accounts it would not only have been fun but would have taught me all that I hadn't learnt about dealing with people, solving problems and making things happen. The trouble was that, as an Irish citizen, they couldn't force me to join unless I stayed on to work in Britain, so it had to be my decision.

At the time I didn't fancy the idea. For one thing, fighting was a serious business; a friend had recently been killed in Korea and another badly wounded, fighting in a faraway land for people of whom I knew nothing. I think, however, that it was another sort of cowardice that was more compelling. I was worried that I might not be officer calibre, and that would be shaming. It cost me dear, that reluctance to join up. My great-uncle, a veteran general of the Black Watch, had hoped to see me in his old regiment. Branding me a coward, not unfairly, he cut me out of his will and promptly died.

Mindful now of what I think I missed, I am a supporter of some form of compulsory social or community service after school for most people. The voluntary schemes, Operation Raleigh, CSV and other gap year options in Britain, or the Peace Corps in America, do a valuable job, but, as always, those who volunteer are usually the people who need it least.

Instead of National Service I joined the Royal Dutch Shell Group and was immediately put on a four-month course. They called it training, not education, but it was not too different from what had gone before, except that now they were paying me rather than the other way round. Our initiation course took us page by page through a thick manual of information about the industry and the company, most of which I wiped from my mind the same evening, having better things to attend to. This was followed by four weeks in a laboratory, a new experience for me, where they demonstrated in miniature how oil was refined, how its viscosity, or thickness, was measured and suchlike technical mysteries.

More information, too much, but since no one knew or had told me where I would be going in the world, or what job I would be doing, it was hard to know which bits of all this data were going to be useful, maybe even vital. Information out of context is only data and soon forgotten. In all this time, the only activity required of us was to light a Bunsen burner or to ask an occasional question.

Seven years later I was given the chance to do something about that. Not quite sure what to do with me after my return from six years in South-East Asia, they appointed me assistant manager of the Group Management Training Centre, responsible for the courses for middle managers from all around the world. That wasn't as important as it sounds; all it involved was arranging for a succession of heads of departments to come down from head office to talk about the work of their units. More data down the drain. I decided that it would be much more interesting for everyone if they had some real problems to work on, problems that I teased out of those head office departments. This was before business schools had been introduced to Britain so I was unaware that I was reinventing the case study.

Not surprisingly, everyone, including the chiefs from on high who came to listen to the groups' conclusions, found this much more interesting. So did I. In fact, I was hooked. I had found my passion – educating adults, using real-life situations as the context for their learning. Thus it was that when Shell decided that it was time, as they put it, for me 'to get my feet wet' again and posted me to run the company in Liberia, I decided that it was time to leave. The new London Business School wanted someone to start their major executive programme. I was ready and willing, particularly when I heard that they wanted me to spend a year at MIT in Cambridge, Massachusetts, brushing up on the American way of educating managers.

I sometimes say, half seriously, that the one thing that I learnt at the Sloan School of MIT was that I hadn't needed to go there, adding 'but I had to go there to find that out'. I went to America convinced that there was a storehouse of knowledge and wisdom in their libraries that they were keeping from us. All I needed to do was to capture some of what they knew and bring it back to Europe. It was a shock to discover that I knew most of it already, having learnt it the long way, by experience. I just hadn't put classy names to it. Like Molière's M. Jourdain, I discovered that I had been using managerial prose without knowing it. Of course, there were some technical tricks and ideas that were genuinely new, but much of it was good sense elevated to academic theory. My time wasn't wasted. I grew enormously in self-confidence. Education for busy managers, I realized, would work only if it connected with their experience.

I returned to the London Business School, which had started just one year before, charged with creating our own version of the year-long full-time programme for mid-career managers, the Sloan Programme, that I had just completed in America. It was a dream commission, were it not for two facts: we had very few teachers in the new school, and no students – unless I could persuade twenty British businesses to release one of their most promising managers, on full pay, for a year, and pay a fee for it. I discovered then, as I made my rounds of the boardrooms, that a one-day seminar was the longest period of management education that any of the people round those tables had ever funded, let alone attended. Most of them thought that I was mad.

In the end, eighteen executives were signed up. Short of conventional business faculty I was free to fill many of their days with my own ideas for their education. I took them to the theatre. Plays, I told them, were case studies of life. There was as much to learn from discussing the themes and dilemmas of *King Lear* as from any study of a family business, and it would be much more exciting as homework. A friend from America, but then teaching at the London School of Economics, led a seminar series that we called Readings in Power and Responsibility, using famous novels and plays as the raw material for discussion.

I shall not easily forget the expression on the faces of these ambitious young executives when they entered the classroom on their first morning to find two texts awaiting them, one entitled Management Accounting, the other *Antigone*, by Sophocles. Values, beliefs and emotions, the stuff at the heart of Sophocles' play, were as important, I argued, as all the numbers for those in responsible management roles. They were subjects that could best be explored and surfaced through great literature. They are the reason that we still queue for Sophocles and Shakespeare so many centuries later. To leave them out of the education of managers is to risk ignoring the humanity at the heart of every organization, and I still believe this to be true.

There is, however, nothing to compare with real life as the context for learning. I travelled with the executives to Communist countries and to America to study organizations there, to compare and contrast them. It was the best that I could do, but I became increasingly convinced that you cannot bring reality into the classroom; all that you can do there is learn to analyse it and conceptualize it better. Because every one of the school's starting faculty had been to graduate schools in America, we had adopted the American tradition of full-time study and we had ignored the British tradition of professional education in subjects such as medicine, law and accountancy. In these professions the classroom was closely tied to practice under supervision. Why should management, such a practical discipline, be different?

The education of managers, I recommended in my 1987 report for NEDO (The National Economic and Development Office), should always be only part-time in the classroom, and accompanied by guided experience in the workplace. I had been much more satisfied with the course that I helped to design and write that started the Open University Business School, a course that forced the students to relate everything to their own current experience where they were working. Only the 'languages' of business, things like accountancy and statistics, marketing and computing, could sensibly be taught on their own, I argued, preferably at the start of a management career. Full-time courses were effectively training people to be analysts or consultants, not managers. By then, however, I had left the Business School.

A couple of years ago I was invited to preside over the North of England Education Conference, the premier conference for the policy-makers and administrators of the state education system. I agreed, on the understanding that I could use the occasion to promote my ideas about education for alchemy, or independence. In my opening address I remarked that many of the alchemists whom my wife and I had studied had been naughty at school. Maybe, I said, we should not be afraid of allowing more naughtiness in our schools. It was the wrong word and the wrong audience. They were horrified at the thought of a growing sea of unruly behaviour in their classrooms. My presidential authority was seriously dented.

They were right, of course. The fact that some alchemists were naughty does not mean that all naughty kids will become alchemists. I had meant only to stimulate debate. What I should have said was that, while order and discipline are essential in any community, we should also encourage more curiosity, initiative and experiment in our schools, without worrying too much if some of the experiments did not work out. They would doubtless have nodded in agreement – and forgotten.

I remain convinced that we should use our schools as safe arenas for experimenting with life, for discovering our talents – we all have some even if they don't show up in examinations – for taking on responsibility for tasks and for other people, for learning how to learn what and when we need to, and for exploring our values and beliefs about life and society. For me, that is a more exciting curriculum than one packed full of facts.

We should also give them golden seeds. Sir Ernest Hall, musician, businessman and social entrepreneur, says that Pablo Casals once wrote:

Why don't we teach our children in school what they are? We should say to them, 'Do you know what you are? You are a marvel. You are unique. In all the world there is no other child exactly like you. In the millions of years that have passed there has never been another child like you. Look at your body. What a wonder it is, your legs, your arms, your cunning fingers, the way you move. You may become a Shakespeare, a Michelangelo, a Beethoven. You have the capacity for anything. You are a marvel.'

PART II

CAPITALISM PAST, PRESENT AND FUTURE

4

THE OLD AND NEW
ELEPHANTS

I had been educated for a world of institutions and corporations, and I set out to join it. I had resolved never to be poor
again and, as I saw it, the way to be at least comfortable
financially was to join a corporation. I was not alone. It was the
age of the organization man, when business offered much of
what one could expect from life – security, prospects of
promotion and the opportunity of fulfilling work. It was a good
life while it lasted but as the borders of the world came down,
communications improved and competition increased, those
corporations were to change radically.

The world of business in which I started has now gone
for ever. The new organizations are already very different
places, and will inevitably have to change even more. In this
chapter I look back to the way things were and forward to the
new challenges the elephants of the future will face.

LIFE IN THE OLD ELEPHANTS

I must still be dreaming, I thought, when I looked up from my cabin berth to see a beautiful Thai girl in a sheer white cheongsam standing above me. 'I'm Donna,' the vision said, 'and I'm Shell. I've come to meet you.' If this is Shell, I thought, then life is going to be even better than I thought. I had arrived in Singapore in 1956, by ocean liner, to start my business life as a trainee marketing executive with Shell Singapore, which in those days covered Malaya and British Borneo.

Donna was just the first example of the tender loving care that Shell, at that time, lavished on its expatriate executives. She was a 'meeter and greeter' who was appointed as my guide and official friend for the first few days until I found my way around. In fact, I was despatched almost immediately to Kuala Lumpur where a company apartment had been allocated to me and another young bachelor. It came as another surprise. I had no idea what a Malayan apartment might be like, but I certainly did not expect it to be the top floor of a lovely old colonial house, set in a garden, complete with gardener and amah, or house servant.

Shell, I was beginning to understand, was what sociologists called a 'total organization' – it encompassed the whole of one's life. They even took pride in fielding their own rugby football team which challenged the winners of the annual inter-state competition. As the newest of some one hundred and fifty expatriates in the company and one of their earliest graduate trainees (a euphemism for someone ignorant of the business and inexperienced in life) I was very much the unnoticed new boy. Until, that is, I happened to score the winning try in a local football derby. The next morning the General Manager greeted me in the foyer of the office: 'Glad to have you with us, Handy,' he said. I had arrived.

But they still did not know what to do with me. I was lucky, however. The manager in Kuala Lumpur was an iconoclast, seen, I subsequently realized, as 'not quite sound'. He thought that the best way to indoctrinate me into the ways of the business and of management would be for me to shadow him for two months. 'Sit in a corner, don't speak when anyone else is here, listen and learn. Come out with me on my tours and visits but keep quiet. And every so often we will discuss your thoughts on what you have seen and heard.'

It was a wonderful introduction into life with one of the elephants of old. I soon realized that I was inheriting an old tradition. Shell, I was constantly reminded, had been around since the turn of the century. The General Manager's house in Singapore was only marginally less grand than that of the Governor-General (Singapore was still a crown colony). I did not need to carry money. It was enough to sign my name and write 'Shell' underneath – they knew where to send the bill and they could be sure it would be paid. There were standards to live up to. Shell was expected to be better than your average company: meticulous, safe and efficient. 'You can be sure of Shell' the hoardings proclaimed and the message was directed as much at us as at the customer. I wasn't just a businessman, it seemed, but a representative of a great organization. It felt good.

Not all of it, however, was reassuring. One evening I met the manager of a rubber estate. In the course of conversation it emerged that he was a not entirely happy customer of our sole competitor and could easily be persuaded to change to Shell. I reported this back to my mentor who was clearly embarrassed. We could not take his business, he told me, unless we had lost an equivalent contract to our competitor. We were, he said, still operating under the old 'as is' understanding of the major oil companies whereby market shares in some regions were kept constant. The rather dubious rationale for what I suspected was illegal was that the stability that resulted allowed for better long-term planning and lower costs for everyone.

I began to worry about those lower costs a week later when, to keep me occupied, my manager asked me to work out next year's prices for all our lubricating oils. I expressed my doubts about my fitness for such a task. 'Oh don't worry,' he said. 'All it involves is getting the cost allocation from the accounts department for each grade and adding on a range of profit percentages that the sales people will give you. It's only arithmetic, I'm afraid.' He smiled.

'But that means,' I said, hesitantly, not quite believing what I was going to say, 'that the higher our costs are, the more profit we make. That can't be fair.'

'That's business,' he replied. 'You'll learn.'

No wonder they were able to look after me so well and still satisfy their shareholders. No wonder that everything we did was done by Shell employees, the drivers, the caterers, even the film unit. That way our standards could be maintained. So what if they cost more; it only added to our profits.

Adam Smith once commented that when two or three men of business are gathered together they are tempted to conspire, but it still puzzled me that otherwise decent people could delude themselves into thinking that it was all right to short-change the public for, as I saw it, the sake of an easy life, or, as they might have preferred to put it, for the benefit of their shareholders. And easy it certainly was out in Malaya in the Fifties, and profitable – until the market grew and new competitors arrived who knew nothing of the 'as is' understanding. Then it was that activities began to be outsourced, costs savaged and margins sliced. But I had moved on by then.

Ever since that morning in the Kuala Lumpur office I have been suspicious of all potential monopolies or oligopolies. I saw then how tempting it was to be in a situation where you were free to set the prices above the costs, however high those costs might be. In a truly open market you are forced to keep the costs below the prices, which are set by the competition. Everyone running a business must privately yearn for the first alternative and to be free from competition, but only unique or superior products can legitimately claim the freedom to set the price they like; and then only for a time, until the competition catches up. I was learning economics the best way, by exposure. Later, I came to understand that what I had experienced was the essence of Karl Marx's analysis: capitalist competition leads to capital concentration. But I hadn't read him then. Since that morning I have been a fervent believer in open competition and open markets as the best guarantors of fairness in every sphere.

I visited Hungary in the old days of the communist regime

when the state ran everything. Why, I asked, in such a small country did they have two fertilizer factories when economies of scale would have surely meant reduced unit costs if there were only one? Because, they said, if there was only one someone in government would have to work out what it should ideally cost to run it, something they would not know how to do. With two factories, each would act as a control on the other. Even under communism, competition was seen to have its uses.

It is a pity, I often think, that governments, who are often rightly intent on privatizing state monopolies, do not pay more heed to that Hungarian lesson. State monopolies turned into private monopolies do no good to anyone except the new owners. Britain's privatization of the railways in the 1990s effectively created a series of monopolies, leaving it to the regulator to look after the interests of the travellers who had no alternatives to choose between. The rail companies were free to set prices above their costs, as long as they could justify those costs to the regulator. Not the best way to run a railroad.

Monopolies are not confined to commerce, as I discovered in years to come when I moved closer to the public sector in a university. There I found that the idea of cost-plus as the basis for pricing or planning was also dominant. Public sector organizations are effectively monopoly organizations, with no check on their costs other than by government inspectors or regulators who, no matter how clever they may be, can have no independent source for checking whether the figures they see are the best obtainable. If the paymaster is the government there is little incentive to experiment with cheaper ways of doing things. That only cuts the income for no discernible advantage. Nobody in government would thank a university president or a hospital administrator for lowering costs – they would merely reduce the budget accordingly.

The good news for the customer, if not for the corporations, is that competition cannot be kept out of the new emerging economy, as the entry barriers to every arena get broken down. Competition will even infiltrate the public sector, with or without the help of governments. In education, health and local government the private sector will increasingly enable more people to buy their way to better service and the public sector will have to respond if it does not want a role as the servant only of the poor. The new companies, in spite of their new size and scope, will no longer be able to prop up their prices in the way that my oil company did all those years ago. Nor will it be possible to organize the big corporations and run them in the comfortable ways of that time.

They were comfortable because they provided us, the employees, with a degree of predictability that is almost unheard of today. They could also plan their own futures. These were the days when long-range planning was in vogue. Rather like farming, one could plan the year ahead although, as in farming, there were always the small emergencies, the bad weather that you could have done without. Later on in my life I was to call them Apollonian organizations.

Apollo, I suggested in my very first book on organizations, was the patron god of the large organization. He was the god of logic and order, of harmony, and also, ironically, of sheep. I was having some fun, at that time, in describing the cultures of organizations and the different styles of management in terms of the gods of ancient Greece. It at least made some use of my classical education, but the initial idea came from my friend Roger Harrison as we sat in the woods of Maine one summer talking about his taxonomy of organizations.

I shall always be grateful to him, because the Greek gods offered me my route to a new career, providing me with what I hoped was a user-friendly method of describing the ways of organizations, why they differed one from the other, and needed to, according to their circumstances. That they needed to be different should have been no surprise, but when I started my studies at MIT's Sloan School of Management I went in the hope that there might be some unifying theory of management, a set of laws for decision-taking and organizing, which would explain all and make management a discipline that could be learnt and then applied. I was doomed to be disappointed. But, I wondered, how else does one get a handle on them if there is no science?

Maybe by pregnant analogy, I then thought, by metaphors that lead to understanding and thence to action. The Greek gods provided the metaphors, and I made them into a book, *The Gods of Management*. There were four gods, enough for my purposes: Zeus who represented the charismatic leader, Apollo representing logic and order, Athena the warrior goddess who symbolized teamwork, and finally Dionysus, to me the god who represented the creative individualist. Each god has his or her strengths. Organizations are always a mix of all four. It is the type of mix that matters.

Twenty years ago Apollo was fashionable. The organization chart, a series of boxes piled on top of each other, was his logo, reductionism his methodology. Take the work of the organization, break it down to its component parts, put those parts in a logical and hierarchical relationship and then, if you have got the logic right and everyone does what their role requires and the manual lays down, inputs will be transformed into outputs with maximum efficiency. It will be a pure bureaucracy, in the best sense of that term.

Organizations, Apollonians think, ideally should be designed like railway timetables, everything slotting together. The assumption behind the timetables is that trains would run on prescribed routes and to time, with no interesting diversions or driver initiatives. There would be emergencies of course and Athenian-style task forces to design new routes and engines. They would need Zeus-type leaders at the top to chart the way ahead and even a few quirky Dionysian creatives in the crevices, but the strength of the organization lies in its Apollonian disciplines, rules and systems of planning and control.

They work well, these Apollonian organizations, when the world in which they live is stable and predictable. Work can be planned, budgeted for and controlled, because the future will not be a projection from the past. They offer careers that can span decades if not lifetimes. Training and experiences can be planned to prepare individuals for programmed roles in the hierarchy. They grow most of their own talent and often generate great loyalty and corporate pride. Shell in my time was like that.

I often compared it to the British army. It even had its own equivalent of regiments; I was in the South-East Asian regiment and I could see that the friendships and connections that I made there would crop up again and again around the group if my career remained with Shell.

Twenty years ago Japanese organizations were the shining examples of Apollonian principles. They promised lifetime employment, but in return they expected obedience, respect for seniors and the acceptance that the organization knows best. They were much admired, but not much fun to work for if you did not happen to be Apollonian by nature. I wasn't and Shell was. That was the trouble. In the first months I already sensed myself to be a misfit.

Eager beaver that I was and keen to learn how things worked, I took it upon myself to look into the transport arrangements for one of our main products, kerosene, used for lighting throughout the country. I worked out that we would save a lot of money if we installed bulk storage facilities up-country and sent the kerosene in large rail wagons rather than by road in small lorries. I wrote it up, put it in a nice folder with a one-page summary at the front and marched into the office of the operations director with, no doubt, a rather smug look on my face.

'I think you will find this interesting, sir,' I said. 'It's a proposal for a new system for kerosene distribution.'

He didn't even look at it. Instead: 'How long have you been with us, Handy?'

'Six months, sir.'

'And how long do you think that we have been in business here?'

'Er . . . Fifty years?'

'Fifty-five, to be precise. And do you really think that in your first six months you are likely to improve on fifty-five years of experience? Now go away and do something useful.'

I did. I devoted myself to my social life, kept my head down at work and put aside any thoughts of contributing ideas to the powers above me. I was a Dionysian trapped in an Apollonian world. I am presenting a caricature of Shell, I realize, but that was the way I saw it then, from the bottom up. Nor was Shell any different from the organizations in which my friends worked. We used to speculate on the oddity that the giants of the free market were themselves centrally-controlled totalitarian states, the antithesis of all that they abhorred politically.

That was forty years ago. Shell is very different now, as are all the current elephants. They had to change if they wanted to survive. Many did not. The *Fortune 500* list of the world's leading companies forty years ago makes strange reading now. Most of those names are not on the list today. They are gone for ever, bust or bought. It is a sign of the times to come that Vodaphone, a company that did not exist in 1981, was for a time, in 2001, Europe's most valuable company, worth half as much again as Shell.

Apollonian organizations find it hard to live in a turbulent world, as the Japanese have discovered recently. It is not that they are averse to change but they like the changes to be incremental, not radical. They like to build on the past, not ignore it. Apollonians talk of planned change and of managing change, concepts that others would think self-contradictory. They like to use the people who have grown up in the organization to manage the new organization, seeking for some continuity to help them through the turbulence.

It never works. It is hard to think outside the box when you are in it. Chekhov's *The Cherry Orchard* was written one hundred years ago, but its moral still works. It is the story of a one-time rich family facing economic ruin. Their one asset, apart from the family home, is their large cherry orchard, now of no commercial value. A business friend suggests to them that they could turn the orchard into an estate of holiday cottages, and so retain their old home. They hardly hear him, the idea is so alien to their ears and their past. In the end, he, the outsider, buys it and they are evicted. Chekhov calls his play a comedy, but it could more accurately be termed the tragedy of our times.

I wondered, in 2000, whether the executives of Marks and Spencer had seen the play. That year M&S, the one-time paragon of retail virtue, was seen to lose its way. Shuffling the top management around did no good. An outsider, a Dutchman, was brought in to take the helm. I suspect, however, that their cherry orchard, all those acres of retail space, will be bought eventually by another outsider and turned into something else. Another Apollonian organization will have found itself unable to think and act outside its own box. In the new mix of gods, Apollo needs his place, although it will never again be the dominant one.

The organizations of today are very different places. That is already clear. But, for all its frustrations, the Shell of my youth had a lot going for it. It would be a shame if the idea of the corporation as a lasting community, the work-time home for many, were to disappear.

THE ELEPHANTS TODAY

For forty years I have watched the organization charts change from a pyramid of boxes to something more like those route maps in airline magazines, a web of lines connecting hubs and nodes with differently coloured lines representing routes flown by partner airlines. I have heard the language change from one of commands to one of contract and negotiation. Organizations are no longer seen as machines with human parts, but as communities of individuals with very individual aspirations. Talent now comes with an individual name tag attached. Customers, too, are people, with names, not anonymous parts of a market segment. Apollo can no longer rule in such a world.

Like most people, I guess, I painted my house – once. I grew my own vegetables – for a few years. I was poor, and I needed to prove to myself that I could do these things. I didn't do them well. In fact, realistically costed, my vegetables probably cost more than those in the local supermarket. For me, these were chores, not leisure activities. Eventually I realized that it made more sense to concentrate on what I did best and pay others to do what they did best. Even if they cost me more per day than I could earn in the same time, I would still benefit if they did the work faster and better than I would have done.

It is no different, nowadays, for organizations.

In the days when I was arguing the case for the shamrock-shaped organization (roughly one-third core staff, one-third subcontractors and one-third part-timers and professional advisers, the so-called contingent workforce), I borrowed a formula that I first heard from the head of a successful multinational: '$\frac{1}{2}$ x 2 x 3 = P, one half of my current core workforce in five years' time, that's my recipe for productivity and profit,' he said, 'as long as they are working twice as hard, and paid twice as much too, but producing three times the value. That way everyone wins.'

'Except for the half that goes,' I muttered, but he didn't hear that.

You can see the formula at work every day. Elephants are marrying or swallowing their one-time competitors and simultaneously slimming down. Banks, oil companies, pharmaceutical, automobile and insurance firms are all doing it. General Electric, the biggest elephant of all, swallowed 1,700 companies in fifteen years under Jack Welch, culminating in the world's biggest industrial takeover, of Honeywell, another conglomerate elephant. But Welch was also known as Neutron Jack because of his unremitting drive to cut layers and numbers out of the organizations that he bought.

Turnover shoots up as a result of the mergers, but staff numbers also tumble down, many of them shunted off into the contractual fringe. The fortunate ones retained in the core find themselves working longer hours but sharing more in the fruits of the enterprise, often with options or bonuses to boost their salaries. If the original companies ever have the time or the information to look back five years they will find that the formula has happened, even though they had never heard of it or planned it that deliberately.

'What happens after five years?' I remember asking the CEO with the workforce formula.

'The same again,' he replied, 'only this time in four years.' Could he be right?

Probably. The old Apollonian companies have, belatedly, discovered that you don't have to do everything yourself if others can do it for you, and do it better and cheaper because it is their speciality.

I say 'belatedly' because some old-established industries have worked that way for ever. Builders, for instance, have always hired in the specialist trades. Publishing has always been a virtual industry: apart from the choice of author everything else could be farmed out, and mostly still is. I sometimes say, only half in jest, that my wife and I are a multinational business, manufacturing in fifteen countries at last count, selling in thirty, with no employees on our payroll and based in a cottage in East Anglia. Of course, we couldn't do it without the help of our 'production partners', our publishers and their 'production partners' down the line. What we produce and own is just the intellectual property, encapsulated in the words and the photographs that we jointly produce.

'Production partners' is the euphemistic term used by Nike for its network of low-cost manufacturers in South-East Asia. Nike is the best-known example of a major virtual company. 'Nike sells concepts,' says Jeremy Rifkind, the American social critic, describing the outsourcing phenomenon in the United States. Although Nike is the world's largest maker of athletic shoes, it owns no factories, machines, equipment or real estate of any significance. What it does have is an information system that ties it all together.

Compaq, likewise, does not manufacture its own computers. Ingram, a company in Santa Ana, California, of whom few will have heard, does it for them, as it does for IBM and any other computer firm that asks them. Ingram will also deliver to the end consumer, even bill them and run a help-line, all under the Compaq logo. Compaq designs the computers, creates the information system that allows the manufacturer to build each unit after receipt of the order, and promotes them through its advertising agents. Like my wife and myself, Compaq keeps a secure hold on its intellectual property but is delighted to farm out everything else to the specialists.

Of course, the really smart idea was to get the customers to work for you, becoming what might be called your shopping partners, and doing it for free. I was in the marketing department of Shell when the idea of self-service petrol stations was first mooted. What a crazy notion, we all thought. Why would anyone want to get out of their car and hold a smelly, dirty hose to fill their tank? We would have to offer big discounts to persuade them. Not at all; the customers were delighted to have control and not to have to wait to be served. No discounts were needed.

From gas stations to the Internet is a small step, conceptually. Now businesses ask their customers to place their orders on their website. General Electric estimates that accepting an order by phone costs $5 to process, but if it comes in online it costs only 20 cents. Thank you, customer, but don't expect a discount. Britain's easyJet airline does offer discounts for reservations done through their website but says that soon it will accept no other form of reservations. No one complains.

There seems to be no logical limit to what can be given out to others to do. New possibilities for unusual partnerships are created. Consulting firms don't just advise any more, they offer management too. In a hint of things to come EDS is offering to run their clients' electronic businesses for them. They will do it for nothing except for a share in the revenue that is generated. The client provides the content, EDS the technology and the management. Each to his own, you might say, and everyone gains. Or do they? Who now is responsible for what? The new dispersed, subcontracted, almost invisible organization is a wonderful excuse to pass the buck if anyone complains.

Franchising is, perhaps, the most visible form of the dispersed organization. It has become the most important new form of business organization since the advent of the modern corporation, says Rifkind. Franchising, he claims, now accounts for more than 35 per cent of all retail sales in the US. Everything you can think of can be, and is, now being franchised – hair salons, driving schools, tutorial services, sports camps, the list is endless. It is fast becoming a lookalike world as the clones multiply in our cities, towns and malls. Not to my taste, I fear. It is, however, one way in which organizations can grow exponentially without employing more people or investing more capital. It also means that thousands of new small commercial enterprises are started each year in every country. Franchises can be schools for fleas, the first step in entrepreneuring.

Going virtual in one way or another is the new management fashion. Get your physical assets off your balance sheet and on to someone else's. Likewise with your employees, get them off your payroll and onto another's. Put your requirements up for auction on the Internet if you want to be sure of getting the lowest price. Unbundle the company. Leave yourself with a design team and an information system and not much else. Except, that is, for the growing problem of managing the new chain of activities and 'partners' – the one thing that is never costed, because we never realize how different and difficult it is going to be. Management becomes, for much of the time, a protracted negotiation between diverging agendas. The danger is that in the rush to bring in the experts you have become one of those hollow organizations that are nothing but a collection of contracts, a name without an identity. Those who don't own something, too often don't care about it. Many good ideas, when carried too far, become liabilities.

The reality, of course, is that organizations cannot look at themselves so legalistically. Like it or not, they are communities of individuals with their own names, individuals who have individual needs, even individual contracts. Those individuals are not 'human resources' or, worse, 'the labour force'. When I returned from South-East Asia to a job in Shell's head office in London I found that all correspondence went, not from me, but from my section, MKR/34. In that Apollonian tower block it mattered not who inhabited MKR/34 as long as that box in the pyramid was inhabited. My name on the office door, I noticed, was on a plastic slip slotted in below the embossed title of the section. In the language of the theory of the day I was clearly only a 'temporary role occupant', not a unique individual. It was dispiriting. My shoulders slumped every morning as I entered that building, facing another day of anonymity.

The more dispersed an organization becomes the more important the trust between some of those unique individuals becomes. It is, they say, the 'R' economy now, R standing for Relationships. The questions are: how many individuals can you know well enough to call them by name, to be confident that you can rely on them or trust them? Between fifty and a hundred, perhaps? Certainly not a thousand. And, how well can you know a person if you have never met them except by e-mail or video conference? I am constantly surprised to be invited to speak at conferences and management get-togethers. Why, in this virtual age, do they need to go to the expense and bother of travelling to some distant resort to watch Powerpoint presentations that they could more easily see in the privacy of their office or home and ask their questions by e-mail? They are there more to meet each other than to listen to me. I am mainly there to legitimate their travel expenses.

Five years ago I went to the Frankfurt Book Fair, something that authors are not encouraged to do because it is too discouraging to see twenty miles of other people's books on display! I was told that I might well be attending the last such Fair, given that electronic communication was so advanced and that book deals could be more efficiently negotiated office-to-office. I haven't been back but I understand that the Fair is now bigger and better than ever. People, it seems, need to meet in the flesh if they are going to have a relationship. Wisely so, if it be true that 70 per cent of a communication depends on eye contact, inflection of tone and body language, leaving only 30 per cent for the actual words.

If today's corporations are going to work effectively they have to create operational units small enough for everyone to know everyone else by name. They will also need to establish face-to-face contact between the key players in the different parts of the airline map. It is not surprising to me, although it sometimes is to the accountants, that the bill for travel expenses in an organization does not decrease as their bill for telecommunications rises, but actually grows. You need to be acquainted with someone personally in order to know whether you can rely on them, even to the degree of understanding what their sometimes cryptic e-mails mean.

I was struck by the relevance of a piece of Sufi teaching I recently came across: because you understand one, you think that you also understand two, because one and one make two, but you must also understand 'and'. The new dispersed organizations are now discovering how much is involved in that little connecting word.

Now the customer, too, has a name, with individual needs and characteristics. There is money in a name. Increasingly it seems that we will pay to be treated as a unique individual. Automobiles are now personalized, made to order and to measure. You can look on a website and see your car being made. Checking in to a Ritz Carlton hotel, I was handed a package marked 'To await Mr Handy's return.' It contained a wash bag that I had left behind six months before. I could have done without it, it was old and shabby, but I was impressed by the apparent thoughtfulness even though I realized that it was all done by computers. Amazon.com and its many imitators bombard you with suggestions tailored to your individual tastes, determined by your past purchases.

This personalization of everything is more than a gimmick. If you think about us as individuals we are, each of us, a potential eighty-year accumulation of cash. Businesses want a share of that. LTV is the new marketing slogan: Life-Time Value. If the business can bond us to itself, it obtains a preferential access to that cash-flow. Knowing your name is just a start. Banks have long given cheap loans to young undergraduates in the hope that they will stay with them when they get rich. Airlines grapple you to them with their frequent-flyer points. Every business strains to create a loyalty to their brand which will lock you into their world. Increasingly you will be offered a product for free, a software programme for instance, in return for your name, address and occupation. You are giving them access to your

LTV and the start of what they hope will be an ongoing personal relationship.

Technology has added force to the new waves of partnership and people, but the surge was coming anyway. The pace of innovation and the pressures of more open markets and keener competition were forcing corporations to be slimmer and more flexible. Ideas and knowledge were also becoming more important than ever in this scene, but these reside in the heads of individuals rather than in machines. The personalization of the corporation and the rise of the unique individual are the result. It means that the new elephants will have to be very different from the Shell I once knew, and more difficult to manage.

The old always has to go to leave room for the new. I look back now with some nostalgia on my days in Shell. No, I didn't fit. But it was a friendly place, much less political, as I later discovered, than academia, which in turn was nicer than the religious world that I entered afterwards. Although at first I rejoiced to think that Shell would take care of my life, I came to resent their assumption that they knew what would be best for me, but it was done benevolently and with proper consideration. The old elephants belonged to an age that is past, but it was in many ways a kinder, gentler age. They will, I suspect, be missed by many who knew them.

THE ELEPHANTS OF THE FUTURE

The old-style elephants may have gone for ever, but large organizations will still be needed, will in fact be more powerful and larger in their reach than ever. Most of us will still be connected with them in one way or another, working with them or for them, selling to them or buying from them, managing them or being managed. Their futures inevitably concern all of us.

They will, however, need to be very different in their ways and habits from the ones we used to know. There are dangerous times ahead for these giants of commerce unless they reform, take those who work for them as seriously as they take those who finance them, and remember that the laws of the market do not take precedence over the demands of justice and ethics.

The new elephants face four major challenges:
1. How to grow bigger, but remain small and personal.
2. How to combine creativity with efficiency.
3. How to be prosperous but also socially acceptable.
4. How to reward both the owners of the ideas as well as the owners of the company.

The First Challenge

In September 2000 Kofi Annan, the Secretary-General of the United Nations, addressed the assembled leaders of the world at the end of the Millennium summit in New York. He concluded that if there was one thing that had been learnt in the twentieth century it was that 'centrally planned systems don't work'. No one walked out. No one commented. It was self-evidently true. The world learns slowly, but ultimately it learns, or rather it unlearns its old dogmas. Likewise organizations. Unlearning, however, good start though it is, doesn't tell you what to do instead.

The big problem facing the new elephants in the decades ahead will be how to manage the long chain of partners of different types and sizes, that airline route map rather than the pyramid of boxes. Add to that the fact that the airplanes on those routes are driven by individuals with minds and aspirations of their own, and you get some idea of the challenge the managers of the elephants face in trying to make sense of it all. The resulting organization is more than a matrix, the consultants say; it is a network, even a complex network. I prefer to call it a federation. It is the answer to the first challenge, the need to be both big and small.

Federalism is a proven way of combining human scale communities with the kind of scaled-up conglomerations that are needed to cope with a world that is, as we are constantly being told, one village, one market, one ecology, one political entity. I am more and more persuaded that federalism is an inevitable organizational form if we are to combine our need for smaller organizations or communities with whom we can identify, and those with enough clout to take on the world. It is, therefore, important that everyone understands what it is and how it works. I am an unapologetic ambassador for federalism, be it in government, in business or in areas such as health, education and the voluntary sector.

Unfortunately, federalism is a political system that is little understood in Britain, or even in America, its most advanced practitioner and the home of *The Federalist* papers, those late-1780s essays which so eloquently spelt out its principles. It is, however, a form of government that is working its way into business organizations as they seek to straddle the world and yet remain small enough to be responsive locally. Where business leads, driven by the need to be competitive, nations and parts of nations will follow. The United Kingdom of Great Britain will one day be the British Federation. Germany and Spain are already federal countries. Italy and France will become ones. Europe will end up as a confederation, a looser type of federation, with up to seventy-five eco-regions, some still linked together as federal nation states. In ten years' time? Probably not, but on the way.

Federalism is not a recipe for centralism, as the British seem to fear. Quite the reverse. It was the preferred choice of the American colonies who wanted no reminders of monarchy, and of the new dominions, Canada and Australia. It is deliberately designed to make sure that no one body can dictate to the rest.

Federalism is, in fact, both centralist and decentralist at the same time, keeping to the centre those functions and decisions that can most usefully be done there but allowing everything else to be carried out by the parts. The trick is to work out which is which. Intriguingly, the centre can be dispersed, allowing some of the parts to undertake some of the functions of the centre on behalf of the whole. The personnel director of ABB in Italy was also at one time responsible for management development across the whole of that huge global enterprise. In the European Union, although it is not properly federalist, individual countries each host some of the pan-European institutions, creating a dispersed centre.

Federalism allows independent units to collaborate without losing their own identity. The idea that sovereignty is indissoluble and cannot be shared is false propaganda. Texas is Texas and also American; Bavaria has its own identity and parliament but is also both German and European. No one in my native Ireland feels less Irish because they are an integral part of the new Europe. Federalism is, therefore, the ideal device for combining partners of all shapes, sizes and ownership patterns in a coherent whole.

The federation, however, is likely to stay together only if the parts are interdependent so that they cannot act as well on their own as they can as part of the greater organization. A collection of separate businesses, a conglomerate, is not a federation and can be dispersed as easily as it was collected. ITT and Hanson were collections presided over by a monarch. When the monarch left, the collection collapsed. General Electric in America has yet to demonstrate that the same won't happen when its monarch, the great Jack Welch, business collector extraordinary, departs. California is the sixth largest economy in the world and could easily stand on its own but it would, amongst other things, have to create its own defence force and its own diplomatic service. It is much better off as part of the United States.

Rather impertinently for a foreigner, I once spelt out the five traditional principles of federalism in an American journal, the *Harvard Business Review*, and interpreted them for organizations. It is important to get them clear in our minds for federalism won't work unless the principles are respected.

First among them is that ugly but crucial word, subsidiarity. Subsidiarity requires that power reside as close to the action as possible. It holds it to be morally wrong for those above or in the centre to steal decisions that properly belong to others. Managers, myself included, too often infringe this principle, demotivating and disempowering those around them. It is the principle behind states' rights.

There are also the principles of twin citizenship, the idea that you can belong to both the smaller and the bigger unit and feel committed to each; the principle of the separation of powers, so that no one group can be both legislator, executive and judge; and the principles of a basic law and of a common currency that hold the whole together.

Federalism is a tried and tested political device. We know how it works and what its snags are. Putting it to work in business organizations is a recognition that these organizations are communities and that the old language of engineering is no longer appropriate. Communities have to be led, influenced and persuaded, rather than commanded. Their citizens demand a voice in their future, want to be trusted and need to be given opportunities to grow.

It is not a model only for business organizations. After I had left Shell and returned from studying at MIT, I found myself, to my surprise, in a federal institution. I was able to experience the phenomenon at first hand. London University is a federal institution with some thirty constituent bodies belonging to it, including such distinguished institutions as the London School of Economics and Imperial College as well as the London Business School where I had come to work. In the Business School we had a great deal of freedom, but in order to use the university's brand, its degree, we had to give up some rights. They retained a few; for instance, the right to veto our selection of students in case they did not measure up to the university's overall standards. At the time I, as programme director, regarded this as unwarranted interference, but that was before I understood federalism. Understanding fosters tolerance.

Britain's National Health Service is an organization inching towards federalism, with quasi-autonomous Hospital Trusts and doctors' practices, held together – too closely together – by a system of rules and a common currency of sorts in which the participating bodies trade their services. That it doesn't work too well is mostly due to the fact that the participants don't recognize that they are part of a federation, a recognized political form with a set of principles.

National voluntary bodies inevitably end up as federal. A central command and control system doesn't work when most of the participants are volunteers, wanting some local voice in what they do. 'I couldn't do with all these branches electing their regional representatives who then elect the national body that tells the rest what to do,' said one head of a notably successful charity. 'The local people knew best what has to be done in their area. My job at the centre was to help them, not to get in their way or to try to do it for them.' There spoke the unwitting federalist. We need more like her.

The Second Challenge

The answer to the second challenge – the need to combine creativity with efficiency – is a requisite amount of alchemy, properly managed. It hardly needs emphasizing that innovation and entrepreneurship are essential to the survival of any organization in such a turbulent time. After studying twenty-one failed civilizations, the historian Arnold Toynbee concluded that their downfall was the result of 'concentrated ownership' and 'inflexibility in the light of changing conditions'. I look at the growing conglomerations of the elephant corporations and worry – can the smaller fry, the fleas, introduce enough flexibility and innovation into the system to keep things from seizing up?

My wife is a portrait photographer, and in 1997 we resolved to collaborate on a joint project. She wanted to meet and photograph creative people, I wanted to try to understand the motivations and backgrounds of entrepreneurs, people who had started organizations, in business, the arts or the community. We decided to call them alchemists, meaning people who create something out of nothing, or turn base metal into gold. The word sounded less brash and thrusting than entrepreneur; it captured some of the idealism that we saw in these people, whatever their field. The project became a book, *The New Alchemists*, with Elizabeth's intriguing 'joiner' portraits which combined different aspects of the same person in one picture, because, she said 'there is always more than one aspect of who we are'. I contributed a short word portrait of the person and his or her life story and life goals.

These alchemists, I realized as I looked at the twenty-seven portraits, were exactly the sort of fleas that the elephants needed to use to keep them dancing. Too many of those who work in elephants are 'In-basket' people, as I was, if I am honest. They are content to deal with the stuff that comes in without attempting anything new. The alchemists, I observed with admiration, didn't react to events, they wanted to shape them, to make a difference. They had three characteristics that made that possible.

First they were passionate. Passion was a word that cropped up in every interview, a passion for what they were doing, whether it was starting a business, creating a theatre company or reviving a run-down community. That passion, the conviction that what they were doing was important, gave them the second characteristic, the ability to leap beyond the rational and the logical and to stick with their dream, if necessary against all the evidence. They also had the negative capability that the poet Keats once spoke of in a letter to his brothers: 'that is when a man is capable of being in uncertainties, mysteries, doubts, without any irritable reaching after fact and reason.' To Keats this was the key to creativity. It needs a certain doggedness, perhaps even arrogance, to hold to a dream against the evidence. This the alchemists all had.

A negative capability, however, would be of little value without the final attribute of the alchemists: a third eye. They looked at things differently. My favourite example was given to us by Sir Terence Conran, famous now as designer and restaurateur. But he didn't start rich. As a young man with no money in London, Terence and a friend resolved to start a low-cost eating house for young people like themselves. This was back in the Fifties when the quality of British food was appalling. Terence volunteered to go to Paris to work as a dishwasher in a restaurant to pick up some secrets of the trade. He came back and told his friend, 'I've discovered one universal truth – chefs are bastards!' Using their third eye, they resolved to create a restaurant without a chef. London's first soup kitchen followed, where a cauldron of great soup was always on the go, with just two men, French bread and what was then only the second espresso machine in London.

But where, I wondered, did they find that negative capability as well as the self-confidence to buck the system, to have a go, to pursue their own dream? Genetics must have had something to do with it, although we failed to find any obvious alchemical antecedents in their personal histories. A childhood in which experiment and small-scale entrepreneurship was encouraged by the parents also seemed to play a part.

More crucially, however, most of the sample had, at some time or other, been given one of those golden seeds that my teacher gave me. Someone whom they respected, a teacher, a first boss, a priest or a godparent, had identified a particular talent and had told them that they were special in that respect. 'When I took my A levels,' one alchemist, Dee Dawson, told me, 'my biology teacher said that I had got the best grades in the whole region. Then I knew that I was clever.' Fortified by this belief she applied to medical school at the age of thirty despite having three young children, got in, graduated and went on to found Britain's first residential clinic for anorexic children.

Finally, we suspected that the alchemists drew strength from a surrounding climate of experimentation and creativity. We had deliberately confined our sample to London, believing that London at the end of the century was a buzzy city, where creativity blossomed. There seem to be clusters of innovation in different parts of the world – Silicon Valley and the Bay area of San Francisco, Barcelona and Dublin in Europe, Sydney in Australia. Some of our sample had moved to London because 'that is where the action is'.

As I listened to the alchemists, I wondered how they would survive working with an elephant. The passion, I felt, came largely from their ownership of the idea, the psychological ownership as much as the legal. Their identity was inextricably tied up with their project, which often bore their name. Could large organizations allow creative individuals the space to experiment and, if successful, the right to be identified with the final product and to have some degree of legal ownership? Could they tolerate the waste created when experiments don't work out as they should? Can the organization learn to plant golden seeds in place of its appraisal interviews?

If the Apollo culture still prevails, the answer to those questions will inevitably be 'only with great difficulty'. In those cultures creativity gets in the way of ordered efficiency. Creativity and experiment are untidy and unwelcome to the logical mind. The federal structure, however, does allow separate units to be innovative without affecting the whole organization, unless and until success has been demonstrated. A federal structure allows an organization to learn from within itself. Clusters of experiment can be cultivated, golden seeds can be sown wherever justified and young people encouraged to be inventive, all without upsetting the ordered progress of the mainstream organization.

Some businesses create their own creative clusters on the margins. Xerox famously established its Parc in Palo Alto, California, but then ignored its best ideas, such as the personal computer. Other people's ideas are not always welcome back at base. Other companies have set up their own internal venture capital bank, making grants to any group that comes up with an idea worth pursuing. J. P. Morgan, for example, has launched what it calls LabMorgan, a $1 billion e-finance unit that will back promising ideas from inside and outside the firm. They hope that it will attract would-be alchemists to join what has been seen as a conservative outfit.

Alternatively, spreading their net wider, businesses ally themselves with research universities in order to exploit scientific developments by faculty and students. Our own study of buzzy cities suggest that it is a combination of research universities with their new ideas, available finance, a thriving arts community, stimulating architecture and a good communications infrastructure which underpins the creative clusters. Organizations cannot by themselves create these conditions, but they can feed into them.

In 1998 Elizabeth and I were invited back to Singapore by the government there to cast an eye over their draft manpower plan. One of their problems, they said, was the need to create a more entrepreneurial culture. Of all the conditions for a creative cluster, only the finance and the communications infrastructure were in place. In that city of four million people there were no professional arts bodies; the first art gallery had just opened but there were still no scientific research facilities at the universities. Singapore was a busy city but not a buzzy one. Their one genuine entrepreneur, whom they paraded for us, had actually started his business in California and Dublin before bringing a part of it back to Singapore.

To their credit, the government had recognized their problem and made a start by changing the priorities of their education system, cutting back the core curriculum by 30 per cent to allow room for experiment. They had built a fine new centre for the performing arts but had no performers as yet to put into it. It was as well, we thought, that their manpower plan was looking twenty years ahead; clusters for creativity take time to build.

A major problem in most countries is the lack of alchemy in government, the biggest elephant of them all. The British government has its central think-tank, called different names by different administrations, but the idea that there might be alchemists in the ministries is an alien one. Civil Servants are naturally averse to risk. Who wouldn't be when accountability means being punished for mistakes rather than rewarded for success and enterprise? Rather than one central 'flea pit', might it not be more productive to create a venture capital hub which would finance experimental projects in any department, thus legitimizing experiment and spreading the buzz beyond the centre? As it is, the lack of any significant internal alchemy provides opportunities for outsiders to start their own idea factories, but without any responsibility or authority for implementing the ideas they are often only fleas dancing in the breeze.

Whole organizations can sometimes become buzzy clusters. The early days of Apple under Steve Jobs were famously creative. It was an organization almost entirely composed of individual fleas aspiring to change the world, a cluster of twenty-something alchemists. They did change a lot; the point-and-click world that we now inhabit was their creation. It went wrong when their success turned them into an elephant. Bill Gates has so far been more successful up in Seattle, turning fleas into millionaires whilst still keeping one of the world's richest elephants roughly on course. The money, these fleas and the alchemists would say, is not the point, but they would nevertheless be reluctant to see others make all the gains from their creativity and drive.

For these reasons, it has so far been easier for the elephants to buy in the alchemists' results when success has been proven, often then spitting out the original alchemist and keeping his or her product. That way the alchemist finds the means to do it or something like it again, for alchemists do not like the thought of retiring. Terence Conran is approaching seventy but his ideas merely get more ambitious. Michael Young, the prince of social alchemists, who has started forty-nine institutions in his time, including the forerunner of Britain's Open University, is in his eighties and three years ago founded his most ambitious project yet, a School for Social Entrepreneurs.

Some have looked to Hollywood for the answer, not to its films but to its way of organizing itself. It has been well described by John Howkins in *The Creative Economy*. Hollywood, he says, is centred around creative people both in front of the camera and behind it, most of them paid by the studio but not employed by it. Today the studios only employ senior management and back-office staff. The rest are independents, often operating through their own personal companies.

The film industry has to be endlessly alchemical. Their core business requires them to produce an endless succession of ideas out of nowhere that can be turned into products. There is no stable state in a Hollywood studio. The producers comb the world for possible subjects for their films, pulling the creative fleas alongside them for a while, to work on a project, maybe in a temporary company, or as just-in-time persons, only there when they are needed. Hollywood also cultivates a buzzy cluster. It is home, as Howkins points out, not only to the world's biggest film industry but to the world's biggest TV production companies, which together support a whole industry of talents supplying everything from the stars to animals and lawyers.

Tellingly, when two Japanese elephants, Sony and Matsushita, moved in to Hollywood, buying Columbia Pictures and Universal Studios respectively, they found themselves out of their depth in this world of fleas and alchemists. As Barry Diller, the successful entertainment entrepreneur, put it, 'The issue of corporate ownership is irrelevant. What is important is the energy, character and entrepreneurship of the individuals. The rest is noise.' Other elephants should take note.

The Third Challenge

As the elephants get bigger, they also become more conspicuous. They then meet the conflicting demands of profitability and social acceptability. It is no longer enough to claim that they pay their taxes and that the rest is up to government.

The elephants may be emaciated, even hollow, in their cores, elongated and stretched across the world, but they still look like colossi to the outsiders. In November 2000, my old friend Shell announced that its profits just for the last quarter were £2 billion. Vodaphone, the newest mammoth, equalled that a few days later, but BP beat it with quarterly results of £2.5 billion. The following week, in the British parliament, the Chancellor of the Exchequer announced that such was the success of the British economy, he could, next year, afford to return £2 billion to the taxpayer in one way or another.

Strictly speaking, the numbers shouldn't be compared because nations don't declare profits, but it is easy to see why many observers think that the big corporations are now both richer and more powerful than many nation states. Nokia is worth more than the GDP of its host country, Finland. People worry that these new corporate states are accountable to no one except their financiers, that they can switch countries at whim, leaving empty factories or warehouses behind, that their financial clout makes governments beholden to them and that their professed concerns for the community or the environment are only gestures. The elephants, people feel, may be out of anyone's control.

It is partly an illusion. For one thing the share of the global economy by the fifty biggest companies has been dropping, not increasing. It went down from 30 per cent to 28 per cent in the five years 1993 to 1998 and is predicted to fall to 15 per cent by 2020. Often, too, the so-called multinationals are not multinational at all, but national companies with overseas operations and partners. Perhaps only ABB, the unusual Swedish/Swiss engineering giant with over 1,500 small operating companies in most countries in the world, could truly be called a multinational organization. Even Shell is still a British/Dutch company at its heart. They are still rooted in their homelands and pay most of their taxes there. They are still within the reach of their home governments and publics.

What concerns a lot of people, including myself, is the way the elephants are marrying or swallowing each other, merging their identities and becoming mere bundles of initials, just like ABB. We have long ago forgotten that ABB stands for Asea Brown Boveri, the names of real people once. Companies used to carry the names of their founders and owners. They stood for something, other than their profits. When they collapse into their initials they are deliberately detaching themselves from their past. In the process they often lose their personality, become anonymous and disappear from our radar screens.

Some, like IBM or GE, rebuild themselves as a brand, but this takes time. It is hard for the general public to trust organizations who decide to call themselves AXA or RSA, Vivendi or Diageo, non-names, one feels, for non-communities. Are they not, we ask, just conglomerations of businesses, bundled together for economic convenience, and as likely to be unbundled again when the convenience is recalculated? Where is the accountability to the rest of us in all that bundling and unbundling?

Equally disturbing are the cultural effects of the cloning elephants, the franchise organizations, the easy way for retail businesses to grow themselves. The paradox here is that in seeking to get closer to more customers the wave of franchising has led to the disappearance of the small personal organization. Our townships have become facsimiles of each other, the same cloned outlets lined up alongside one another. We are Starbucking the world. The demonstrations against globalization in 2000 were as much about the cultural contamination that globalization has brought as about the power of the international bodies like the World Trade Corporation or the International Monetary Fund.

Justified or not, perceptions matter, as those demonstrations proved. Customers and would-be employees are becoming more choosey. In 2001 there were over a hundred hot sites on the Internet slagging off individual corporations. Monsanto ran into a storm of abuse when it sought to sell its 'suicide seeds', which don't reproduce themselves, to the farmers in the Third World, meaning that the farmers could no longer save seeds for the following year but had to buy new ones. Monsanto lost the battle and their good name. Reputations matter and brands are fragile things, as Shell found out to its cost in the Nineties after being accused of defiling the environment in the North Sea and trampling on human rights in Nigeria. Who would have expected motorists in Germany to spray bullets on Shell petrol stations in protest against that company's actions in the North Sea and Nigeria?

The managers whom I know in Shell and other companies are decent individuals, not out deliberately to exploit anyone or anything, people who in their private lives share a concern for the environment and for the poor of the world. But 'we took a hard look at ourselves as a company', Shell bravely declared, 'and didn't like much of what we saw'. They understood that they must work harder not only to be good, but to be seen to be good. Social responsibility has to be redefined by the big corporations. It is not about giving a little of your profits to the poor. It is not about how much money you make and what you do with it. It is about how you run your business and how you balance the requirements of the different interest groups.

Environmental and social audits made public and a triple bottom line that measures progress on environmental and social criteria as well as financial are becoming standard practice among the leading companies. Prodded, apparently, by a group of its young executives, BP/Amoco has announced that BP now stands for Beyond Petroleum. A touch too good to be true, perhaps, and BP has yet to put some substance behind its fine words, but it is an indication that the new workforce wants a purpose for their time and their work that is more than increased shareholder value. They want to think that they are helping to make the world a better place. Companies can no longer buy respectability by a bit of philanthropy. Increasingly we want to know *how* they make their money as well as how much they make. They cannot turn over as much money as whole countries and not expect to be held accountable for the way they do it.

Recently the British government has required pension fund trustees to state their ethical values in their reports and may well include a similar requirement in a revised Company Law. This kind of formal accountability can only help to remind those in charge of businesses that they are more than just a money-making machine. They are also a community within other communities and have to earn the right to operate. The corporate leaders that I know welcome these legal requirements because they put the onus on their competitors to do as they do.

In the end, however, corporations will be held to account for their public actions more by their customers and their employees than by their shareholders, helped by pressure groups such as Greenpeace – and by the consciences of their leaders. In Britain there is, every year, a 'Take Your Daughter To Work' day. The idea is to give the daughters a taste of what work means, but it can work the other way. Discussing their day together, one daughter, a bright fourteen-year-old, said that she had been surprised by some of her father's priorities; 'Not the way he would have behaved at home,' she said. The father was taken aback, but he did admit that the person he was in the office was not always the same person he was at home. 'Maybe,' he laughed, 'I ought to employ her to keep me true to myself.' We shouldn't need our daughters to make sure that we bring our true selves to work.

The Fourth Challenge

Intellectual property – the ideas, skills and knowledge that drive the company – is now recognized as the key asset of most organizations. We can no longer expect the owners of this property, the individual employees, to be so ready to concede all their rights of ownership to the company in return for a contract of employment. Their rights must be balanced against the rights of the legal owners of the business, the shareholders.

The old world knew what property meant. It was something that you could see and measure. You could sell it, rent it, use it, even destroy it – if you owned it, that is. You can't do all those things to intellectual property, even if it takes the form of a patent or a copyright. I can't destroy your idea, even if I buy it from you, because you still have it. As accountants know only too well, the only way that you can put a monetary figure on intellectual assets is by subtracting the value of the physical assets from the market's estimate of the value of the total company. Defining things by gaps in other things is never very satisfactory; it suggests that those things aren't really there, that they are just ghosts in the machine. This invisibility may account for the muddle about the new sort of property, for how can anyone claim to own something that often can't either be seen or counted? As W. Edwards Deming, the total quality guru, pointed out, 97 per cent of what matters in business can't be counted.

Not that people aren't trying these days. David Boyle, in his book *The Tyranny of Numbers*, lists a few of the devices – GIPS, TOMAS, EFQM and BREAM are just some of the acronyms. There are new social auditing standards SA8000, GRI and AA1000. Some academics have even attempted to measure culture numerically with eleven metrics. One suspects, however, that all these well-meaning attempts will only prove Deming to be right. What really counts can't be counted, or, as Thomas Stewart of *Fortune* puts it, 'it is easier to count the bottles than describe the wine.' Not only is it intangible, this new property, it is also fragile. 'Reputation, reputation, reputation', exclaimed Othello after his one disastrous mistake, 'O, I have lost the immortal part of myself, and what remains is bestial.' It is a lament that companies such as Union Carbide after Bhopal, or, indeed Monsanto and Shell, must have echoed as one mistake or disaster dented their reputation – and their share price.

So it is that intellectual property in all its different forms will become an increasingly hot topic among the new elephants in years to come if they do try to grow their own alchemists. In particular, the originators of ideas are going to demand a share of the results. Why, they ask, should all the profits go to shareholders who only contribute their money, not their time or their skill? Why should a contract of employment necessarily mean that everything I come up with during the period of that contract belongs to the employer?

I can envisage alchemists being treated more like myself as an author, demanding and getting a share of the income stream resulting from their work, perhaps expressed as a share of the equity or as options, but negotiated in advance. Personally, I would rather have a share in my books' income stream than a bet on the future share price of my publishers, something that I cannot influence in any way. Already, it is thought, some 30 per cent of the equity in American companies is tied up in promised stock options. This is cheap remuneration because it is not charged as a cost in the accounts of the business. It is, however, a risky and dubious way of rewarding talent.

As the economist John Kay has pointed out, Bill Gates currently holds 25 per cent of Microsoft shares and his employees another 15 per cent or so. If the stock rose by 10 per cent a year above its present levels the employee stockholders would see the worth of their stock rise by some $7 billion, almost exactly equivalent to Microsoft's profits. If that sum were to be charged as employee remuneration the profits would disappear. If the price of rewarding alchemy means many more of these free options, the owners, the proper shareholders, who have paid real money for the risk they bear, may start to revolt.

But then, what does it mean any longer to say that shareholders 'own' a business when so many of its assets are intangible and invisible, often contained in the heads of people who could walk off with them at a day's notice? When the Board of Saatchi & Saatchi sacked Maurice Saatchi from the company that bore his name, he left obediently, but took with him the accounts of British Airways and Mars, as well as some key staff. The stock promptly halved in value and the Saatchi & Saatchi shareholders found that they really only owned half of the company. It was never very clear, anyway, what shareholder ownership meant. Owning a share in Shell didn't mean that I could demand to use its offices, or ask it to lend me money in an emergency. Nor could it mean that I owned the people in the company. They aren't my or anyone else's slaves, only employees with rights defined by law and contract.

My guess is that we shall, eventually, have to abandon the myth that shareholders own a business. They will be more like mortgage holders, entitled to a rent for their money, in this case a variable rent depending on the profits, but with no rights to sell the company or to close it down, unless it defaults. The shareholders contribute their money. Others contribute time, skills, ideas and experience. These, too, are entitled to a rent, variously fixed. No one owns anything. The very idea that a collection of people turning ideas into products is a piece of property that can be owned by someone else will come to seem absurd.

Crude economics will, as ever, be the lever of change. There is already an abundance of capital. In 1999 US companies received $50 billion in venture capital, twenty-five times as much as in 1990. Companies launched on the stock exchanges received $70 billion new finance, fifteen times the amount in 1990. One reason for the booming American stock market in the 1990s was this abundance of money looking for a home. Even if the stock markets of the world dip, that money will still be out there. As a result, shareholders won't have so much power. Ideas, not money, will be in short supply.

Meantime, more and more people are going to become aware

that their knowledge has a marketable value. They will be reluctant to sell it for a time-based contract, a wage or salary. They will want to charge a fee or a royalty, a percentage of the profits. The difference is that a salary is money paid for time spent, whereas a fee is money paid for work produced, irrespective of the time spent on it.

Employees are paid wages or salaries. Independents charge fees. The independent sells the result of his or her know-how, but not the know-how itself. The employee, by selling time not results, has implicitly sold the know-how needed to turn that time to profitable use. I feel certain that we shall see more and more independents charging fees to organizations in order to retain control of their knowledge. More of that elusive intellectual property will then belong to the fleas and be only on loan to the elephants.

Ricardo Semler gives the employees of his maverick company, Semco, in Brazil, the choice of eleven different ways to be paid, ranging from a fixed salary to a variety of royalty schemes, commissions, stock options and targeted bonuses, any of which can be combined in a huge array of possibilities. Semco, in fact, even though it employs 2,350 people is really a loose federation of groups of fleas, with the centre acting as a mixture of venture capitalist, mother hen and consultancy. The company carries its faith in people to what some would think impractical extremes, but more and more organizations will have to follow its lead and treat people as separate individuals, not as homogenous human resources, and pay them accordingly.

The mechanism could be the incorporation of individuals. John Birt, when he first joined the BBC as its Director General, came under a contract signed with his personal company, not as a salaried employee. He was ahead of his time. The Corporation and the world outside were horrified. In ten years' time it will be normal practice for anyone who believes that they have a marketable talent or skill. There will be individual contracts for individuals negotiated with their personal companies, no doubt through their agents or lawyers. What is already the norm for actors, and even for authors, will be commonplace; maybe a nightmare for organizations but a field day for lawyers. In a world where the fleas hold the property that matters, the elephants will have to adjust their ways if they want to keep the best. Semler boasts that the staff turnover in his company during the last six years has been less than 1 per cent.

Organizations as federations of groups of fleas? Some believe that we all want to work and live that way, independent yet belonging to something more than ourselves. Nigel Nicholson, a professor at the London Business School, argues in his book *Managing the Human Animal* that we are 'hardwired' by our inheritance from our prehistoric ancestors to want to behave in certain ways. 'You can take the manager out of the Stone Age but not the Stone Age out of the manager' is the way he puts it. In this neo-Darwinian view of the world the ideal organization would have small units, a flexible hierarchy and leadership, working mostly in team projects but recognizing the individual; diverse, but with high trust and high involvement; self-critical but with rewards that recognize personal achievement. Wouldn't we all like that?

Perhaps we are naturally inclined to be fleas of one sort or another, shoved against our instincts into logical boxes by our organizations, persuaded by our schooling to elevate reason above human nature. If so, then the economic pressures that will force the elephants to treat more and more of their people as individual economic units will end up by aligning our organizations with the grain of human nature, to the benefit of everyone. Unless something like that happens we may see the tables turning and the holders of the intellectual property, the key employees, holding the corporations to ransom. In a bizarre way, Marx's desire and prophecy, that the workers should control the means of production, will have come true.

5

THE NEW OR
NOT-SO-NEW
ECONOMY

We all, elephants and fleas both, operate against the background of what is going on in the economy as a whole. The Internet, and the possibilities it gave birth to, tempted many to predict a new kind of economy, one of endless flexibility and limitless growth. For a time the relentless growth of the American economy, boosted by developments in the new technologies, seemed to support their ideas. The reality, as so often, is less Utopian. The new economy turns out to follow some old rules: profit cannot be postponed indefinitely and share prices go down as well as up. The new technologies have, however, brought us many new facilities and exciting new tools. Some of what we are seeing is the old world in new clothes. It may intrigue us for a time but it won't change the world. Some is really new with radical implications.

THE NOT-SO-NEW ECONOMY

There is some truth in the observation that any changes in technology that occur before we are five years old are taken as the norm; changes before the age of thirty-five are seen as exciting, opening up avenues to new possibilities, but changes after thirty-five can be upsetting and disturbing. Young children, therefore, take computers and mobile phones in their stride. The e-revolution, if that is what it is, tends to be led by entrepreneurs in their twenties, while the older generation usually remains more suspicious.

As someone at the end of his sixties I am unlikely to be one of the uncritical enthusiasts for the new technology. We cannot and should not stop technological change because it is one of the fruits of human creativity, nor is it reversible. Much of this change, however, we will absorb into our routines, after a brief period of bewilderment or excitement, and go on living and working as we always have done. Self-reordering fridges will be commonplace, no doubt, as will watches that not only tell you the time but also where you are and how to get to where you want to be; but they won't alter our lives.

Forty-four years ago I started my business career in Kuala Lumpur as a marketing assistant for Shell. It would be three years before I saw Britain again, because it took so long to make the journey. Come Christmas, I thought that it would be nice to ring home in Ireland. That was not a simple procedure. You had to book your call some weeks ahead and when the time came and you were asked to pick up your phone, you heard the call relaying its way from operator to operator across the world. 'Bombay calling Cairo – I have a London call for you' and so on until the call reached our local exchange in rural Ireland and I heard Mrs Jones, our postmistress come on the line.

'Is that Mr Charlie?' she said. 'Your parents know you are going to call. It's awful weather here. What's it like where you are, wherever that is?'

'Please Mrs Jones,' I said, 'it's lovely to hear you but I'm only allowed five minutes and I do want to speak to my parents.'

She put me through, grudgingly. It wasn't every day she got to chat to someone across half the world.

These days our daughter works in New Zealand. We e-mail her most days, speak on the telephone once a week for half an hour at a cost of only £1 and meet twice a year at least, here, there or halfway. It is only when I look back to those beginnings that I realize what an extraordinary revolution there has been in communications. The remarkable thing is the ease with which we have all taken the changes in technology in our stride, and I suppose that one day it will be as commonplace to go on a space ride as it is today to hop on the Eurostar from London for lunch in Paris. Technology has shrunk the world but has it really changed it?

I have also been struck by the lure of these technological changes. Because something exists we are tempted to use it. Because it is now possible to fly from Kuala Lumpur to London for a meeting, people do. Because we can copy a message to half the organization at the click of two keys, we do. Because it is possible to do business around the globe around the clock, we do. And exhaust ourselves. My first independent command was running Shell's marketing company in Sarawak. There was no telephone line to the regional head office and my bosses in Singapore. We managed because we had to.

And maybe it was better, because there was no real way they could judge me other than by the results. Things had to be pretty worrying for anyone to spend two days coming to visit me in what was not the most luxurious of places. I was young, twenty-four, and hardly knew the difference between gasoline and kerosene but I learnt fast. If I made a mistake I at least had the chance to correct it before anyone noticed. That might not be possible today without a lot of self-discipline by superiors. Fewer mistakes, maybe, but less learning, less responsibility.

The early days of e-tailing or B2C (business-to-customer) have not been as soaringly successful as the techies suggested it would be. If it is information or advice that you are buying, or its offshoots such as airline tickets, hotel reservations or stocks and shares, things that can be delivered through your screen, then the system works reasonably well, although there are still doubts about secrecy and privacy that have to be assuaged. If it is something that has to be delivered physically, then we find that we are thrust back into the old world of people putting things into boxes, driving vans, turning or not turning up on time. It will be no different from old-fashioned mail order, or from the days in my parents' Irish rectory when my mother rang the grocer in Dublin once a week and his van arrived every Friday morning, usually with at least one item missing 'out of stock', and another misunderstood.

Behind the glitz and the early excitement the real management problems of the early dotcoms turned out to be much the same as those that have always faced new organizations. Designing a website is a new sort of fun, but the founders of the business still have to turn their initial idea into a proper business plan. They have to hawk it around to potential angels, banks and venture capitalists who will be sceptical, cautious and reluctant to part with good money for a dream, just as they have always been. That achieved, there are the necessary disciplines of marketing and advertising the site, the even drearier problems of warehousing, distribution and call centres to attend to, all of which involve the old traditional areas of recruitment, logistics management and training.

I listened to one of the founders of the early British auction site, QXL. The real problem, he said, was nothing to do with the business idea or the technology; he was perpetually frustrated because the staff would not get into the office on time in the morning. Another e-tailer told me that her main difficulty lay in motivating the young people who manned the call centre in the north of England, who found themselves doing a boring job in a glamorous industry but where the glamour never rubbed off on them. A staff turnover of 30 per cent in a year costs money, money that was not in that original business plan. Or as another dotcomer told me, 'My mistake was to think that youthful enthusiasm could make up for lack of experience. I had to get rid of everyone I started out with.'

Another start-up success could not tell me which bits of the business were generating profits and which were running at a loss. Financial controls, she said, were just something they had been too busy to get around to. Her backers, she complained, kept talking about her 'burn rate' – the time when her money would run out. 'They have no faith in our future or in me.' I sensed that they might be right to be worried. The management of people and money remain the essential preconditions of success in the e-world. *Plus ca change, plus c'est la même chose.* The new new world will need the old old skills as well as some of its own.

The Economist magazine ended a survey of e-business with a review of the ten skills needed to manage the new businesses of the e-world, based, it said, on the many writings on the subject. Summarizing a summary, it went like this:

1. Speed. Everything happens faster. Bureaucracy stifles decisions.
2. Good people. They need to be fewer but better.
3. Openness. Transparency pays.
4. Collaboration. Teams are the building blocks.
5. Discipline. Protocols and standard procedures are the keys to efficiency.
6. Good communications. People need to know eveything that is going on.
7. Content management. Eighty per cent of information is unnecessary.
8. Customer focus. Treat every customer as an individual.
9. Knowledge management. Share what you know.
10. Leadership by example. Practise what you preach, get online.

I was underwhelmed by the list. The order might have varied a little, but it was the same list that I had been urging on organizations and their managers for thirty years. Management in the e-world remains a matter of common sense. It's doing it that is difficult.

As I wondered just how new it all was, I listened to Tom Standage, author of *The Victorian Internet*, as he pointed out in a discussion at the Royal Society of Arts that we have been here before. In the 1840s the electric telegraph was invented. The resulting telegraph network, which was likened to a spider's web, grew with exponential speed. It spawned new firms and business models and led to an acceleration in the pace of business life that has not been equalled since. Companies had no choice but to embrace the new technology; there were complaints of information overload and encroachment on family life. New forms of crime emerged, which led to the development of codes and ciphers. Telegraphers communed in chat rooms, telling jokes, swapping gossip and playing chess. Inevitably, romance blossomed between operators in distant cities.

There was, said Standage, no shortage of telegraph hype. 'All the inhabitants of the earth', someone declared, 'would be brought into one intellectual brotherhood.' Pundits proclaimed a new era of peace: 'It is impossible that old prejudices and hostilities should any longer exist,' said one, 'while such an instrument has been created for the exchange of thought between all the nations of the earth.'

Alas, it did not work out that way. The world soon adjusted to its new baby and went on much as it always had. Today, you could say that we are only seeing an improvement in communications technology, one which we will also take in our stride. The Victorians, Tom Standage concluded, would be impressed by aeroplanes but would regard the Internet as old hat. All in all, as Bill Gates has been honest enough to admit, in comparison with such essentials as basic health care and nutrition, universal Internet access comes pretty far down the list of priorities.

There was an advertisement running in *The Economist* by a group of private bankers in Geneva. It was headed, 'We've been working *online* for 200 years; in other words talking directly with our clients.' They went on to proclaim, 'It goes without saying that we can master the most up-to-date data and communications technologies … But these technological innovations are only there to reinforce the human relations values of confidence, proximity and responsiveness, that are the very essence of our business.'

The implication behind their promotion is important. To a large extent the new technology reinforces what already happens. It doesn't replace it. Most of the occupations that we are familiar with today will still exist in twenty years' time. They will be enhanced by the new technology, of course. There will be satellite navigation in the cabs of every lorry, for instance, but there will still be lorries – more of them, probably, delivering all those goods that we ordered through the Internet from our armchair instead of going down the high street or to the shopping mall for them. Behind the website of every e-tailer there has to be a warehouse and a delivery system, and at the beginning of every book downloaded onto an e-book there is still an author. Plumbers and electricians may be more hi-tech, but they will still exist, as will doctors, nurses and, naturally, lawyers, together with most of the current professions. Our kitchens may well be so automated that designer meals can be set cooking with a coded message from our mobile phone, but I suspect that we shall still eat out, for the richer we are the more we buy the pleasure of the experience as much as the goods.

The experience economy, as it is called, the money that is spent on going to the theatre, on recreational travel, eating out or going to a football match, has long since overtaken the physical economy. In 1980 some 287 million people took international trips. By 2020 it is thought that 1.6 billion or 20 per cent of the world's population will be doing so. Clever marketing seeks to turn even the most mundane activity into an experience. Shopping is now an excuse for a family outing. Airlines no longer offer just to transport the busy executive from here to there but to give him a relaxing space for sleeping, working or entertainment. 'Come and enjoy the experience of travelling with us' they are saying, because in the experience economy firms are selling memories, not goods. On the plausible assumption that we shall have more disposable income twenty years hence, this experience economy seems likely to grow as we look for something other than mere objects to spend our money on.

It may be enhanced by the new technology but it will always be a people-centred part of the service economy. Indeed, the tendency is that the more you pay for the experience the greater the number of people who need to be involved. Smart hotels boast of the numbers of staff they deploy per guest to cater for all their whims. If technology makes our societies richer we may, paradoxically, end up with more people employed in personal relationships rather than fewer, doing much what servants have always done but now with more dignity because it is done as a business for profit and not as a duty. One hundred years ago cooks, drivers, cleaners and gardeners were classified as 'domestic servants'. They were the largest group in the employment statistics. There is no longer such a category in the statistics but the drivers, cooks and cleaners are still there for those who can afford them, only now they are independent businesses, 'Cooks Unlimited' or 'Chauffeurs for Hire'.

As societies grow richer they often return to more organic products and environmentally friendly ways. Handmade becomes upmarket, traditional is good. The craft workers and new-style artisans may use their mobile phones to check back with their base, or even to look up their stock prices, but the work they do is much as it has always been down the centuries and I expect it will continue, even revert to what is older still. Take the small annexe we have been building on to our country cottage. For good environmental reasons we are making the walls out of hemp. Mixed with lime it provides wonderful insulation and fire protection and also cushions any noise. Besides that, it looks nice, with a natural texture, and because it grows in the field it is ecologically pure. The hemp/lime mixture, however, has to be packed by hand between timber supports until it hardens. It is very labour-intensive and old-fashioned, a building process not unlike that with which the Tudors built their timber-framed houses back in the sixteenth century.

Some manufacturers have even concluded that the way to people's pockets is more likely to be found by providing an all-inclusive service experience than through the straightforward marketing of their goods. Products are hiding their faces behind offers of personal service. Hewlett Packard offers advice and consultancy, backed by its boxes of computer hardware. Unilever is experimenting with a household cleaning service as a way of getting its cleaning products into our houses. Shell has set up an experimental laundry in order to boost the sales of its chemicals. You are encouraged, now, to lease your carpets as well as your autos. Don't buy an air conditioner, buy an air-conditioning service. Ownership is a bore, access is what matters, says Jeremy Rifkind in *The Age of Access*.

Computers add gloss to the experience by personalizing everything, so that every message from anybody, be it on your screen or in your mail, will have your name on it, but no one is deceived; to make it truly personal there has to be a person in touch with a person. Moreover, behind every experience there has to be a nugget of something solid. Theatre would be an empty experience without a play, shopping a frustration if there was nothing to buy. Content is key, they say, and in the information age, where knowledge and ideas will provide most of the content, we shall need individuals to provide that content. Elephant organizations may control the technology, where economies of scale and deep pockets are needed, but without content they are ultimately worthless. AOL was nothing but a way to access the Internet until it bought Time Warner and all the content that firm owned, content that needed a way to reach the world. Content is ideas made tangible, and ideas stem from individuals, alone or in groups.

Talent, therefore, is precious, as it always has been, but in future it will be more so. Golden hellos are growing in size, yet not every talented flea will want to sell their intellectual property to an elephant. Four young men, escapees from a traditional corporation, had launched an innovative dotcom business in London only to find that to reach its full potential it needed finances beyond their scope. They needed to sell it on to a big player. One company told them that they were not interested in the business but would love the four of them to come and work for them. The company offered to pay them half a million pounds up front if they joined, some of which they would need to use to pay off their original backers. The four refused. Their freedom was more precious.

It is even possible that the e-revolution has been over-hyped. There was certainly a degree of 'irrational exuberance' in the early days of the dotcom launches. This cooled off within a year or so, when the stock market concluded that annual sales multiplied by the growth rate was not the best way of valuing a business if profits ultimately failed to materialize. Nasdaq, the American stock market for hi-tech stocks, doubled in 1999 only to fall back the next, heralding, it seemed, the end of America's long boom. Only the companies that were offering genuine technological innovations survived the cull and even they were battered. Cisco, in 1999 the world's most valuable business, saw its share price fall by 80 per cent two years later. Its chief executive observed at the time, as he announced the sacking of 17 per cent of his workforce, 'this may be the fastest any industry our size has ever decelerated.' Moreover, as people are slowly realizing, not everyone needs or wants to change their mobile phone or their laptop every time a new model comes out. Markets get saturated as they always have done. The new technologies are not immune.

In 2000 Britain's and Germany's mobile phone companies competed in an auction for the right to licences for the third generation of mobile phones, the WAP phones, bidding over £20 billion in both countries. That equates to a start-up-cost of maybe £2,000 per subscriber, which will have to be recovered with interest. *The Economist* reckoned that the phone companies of Europe were facing a total investment of around £300 billion to launch the new phones, all of it eventually to be recovered from their customers.

No one knows whether people, having got used to calls of less than 1p a minute on existing phones, will be prepared to pay quite a lot more for the privilege of surfing the web while they walk. None of the companies, however, felt that they could afford to be left out of what might be the future but it may yet prove to have been a risk too far. It might seem convenient to have the web in your pocket on a tiny screen, but when all the excitement dies down it is still a tiny screen. One unexpected result of new technologies has been to turn telephony into a commodity business, a world of low margins where brands don't matter.

Meantime we have already absorbed the existing technology and taken it in our stride. It is hard to believe that the web is only ten years old. Who would have thought that grannies would be surfing it and would delight in e-mailing their offspring – no fear now of interrupting their loved ones at inconvenient moments, and replies are almost guaranteed, even from the most dilatory of grandchildren.

Nowadays I get business cards with only an e-mail address and a website, for some people seem to live in cyberspace, a word itself unknown twenty years ago (it was coined by William Gibson in 1984 in his science fiction novel *Neuromancer*) . You can make a model of yourself at Gap's website, dress it in clothes of your choice and even turn it around to see yourself from the rear. We now have a digital mail order catalogue of infinite possibilities, if that's the way you want to shop.

We also have a worldwide friendship network to join or leave at our choice. Love on the Internet is fancy-free, and risk-free. Adultery without pain or hurt! We can join clubs without the fear of being blackballed, be the sort of person we can only dream of being in the physical world, reinvent our character over and over again, live ten lives in ten days if we so wish. Reincarnation on demand!

A friend, in her sixties, spends her days connecting a world-wide network of animal rights campaigners, all from her cottage in an English country town. 'People speak more frankly on e-mail,' she says. 'I've made so many friends all over the world.' More than that, we can tell our politicians what we think of them, literally as they speak, putting the people truly in power, democracy made real at last. The whole wide world literally at one's fingertips is a wondrous thought, liberating, mind-expanding, exhilarating; but once the initial thrill has passed will we really want the responsibility and the workload that goes with the opportunity?

Organizations are finding that the Internet is not just a new way to communicate. It is a market-place where they can put orders out for bids, it is an instant newspaper for its staff, it is an ever-open order facility for its customers plus an endlessly updated inventory of those customers' likes and dislikes. In theory, it reduces the costs of every business process that involves information, be it a plan, an advertisement, a set of accounts, a request for supplies or a schedule of deliveries. Organizations don't have to own everything any more, they can be virtually integrated instead, connecting the different bits and pieces through this new medium. B2B, or business-to-business, is, they say, the real future of the Internet and it will transform our organizations, with firms like Oracle and GE talking of saving up to 10 per cent of their costs over two years. I wonder, however, if they are not underestimating the cost of 'and' in that Sufi maxim, for the lowest bidders are not always the best partners.

THE NOT-SO-GOOD NEWS

It is early days. It took around thirty years after electricity was invented for the full effects to appear. Thus far the e-revolution has spawned a lot of new toys and some improved efficiency, but it is not all good news. For one thing there is too much of it! One American consultancy firm found that many of their executives were receiving a hundred and fifty e-mails and over a hundred voice-mails every day. Three hundred e-mails a day is not uncommon, and most recipients want to scroll through them all themselves even though it takes them a good hour every day. Go away for a week and one thousand of the things will await your return. No wonder, then, that so many take their laptops to the beach or that 'sleep camels', as they call them in Silicon Valley, those who sleep only at weekends, are becoming more common.

The European Commission calculates that 'spam', unsolicited junk e-mail, is costing Internet users £6 billion a year, most of it in wasted time. 'Our people have stopped thinking,' another top executive complained to me. 'They are too occupied in responding.' Secretaries may be disappearing from the executive suite only to be replaced by a new breed of information gatekeepers. But even they may not be able to keep insidious invaders at bay. A virus wiped out my address file the other day and lost half an essay. And the mail that does get past the gatekeepers, human or electronic, seems to demand an instant response. Friends phone me to ask if I have received their e-mail of the day before because they had received no reply.

David Grayson of Britain's Business in the Community has come up with a neat summary of the pace of change. All of the world's trade in 1949 happens in a single day today, all the foreign exchange dealings in 1979 happen now in a single day, as do all the telephone calls made around the world in 1984. A year in a day is exactly how it feels sometimes. Slow down this digital world, I sometimes cry, or at least give me a pause button.

Then again, neither speed nor quantity is any guarantee of quality, or of truth. The Internet screens out age and gender, which may be politically correct but if you don't know who is typing or talking the veracity has to be dubious. My friend wanted a medical definition of death. Instead of looking in the dictionary he posted a note on the web. 'Amazing,' he said. 'Within an hour I had ten replies.' 'Were they all the same?' I asked. 'No,' he replied, 'of course not, it's a dicey question.' 'So how do you know which is the best since you know none of the respondents?' Answer came there none!

More sinisterly, the Internet can be a playground for paedophiles. A man of forty-seven was convicted in England of having sex with a thirteen-year-old girl whom he first corresponded with on the Internet, concealing his age until she agreed to meet him. In the financial world, anyone can now lay claim to insider knowledge of companies and try to hype a share price in order to make a quick profit; 'pump and dump' the Americans call it. In February 2000 a small British coffee roasting company called the Coburg Group, valued at £2.5 million, saw its share price multiply seven times on the rumour that it was about to launch an Internet venture. When the board denied the rumour the price dropped back but by then the pumpers had probably taken their profit and dumped their shares.

Or take products: you may be able to read and see the items in the catalogue but touch them and feel them, smell or taste them you cannot. I like to press my avocados before I buy them to make sure they are ripe. If I order by Internet I have to trust the store's assertion. Already we seem to trust brands more than individuals, because we don't get to know individuals well enough.

Europeans love their mobile phones because at least there seems to be a human at the other end. But mobile phones also herald a change in the way we organize ourselves because now a phone belongs to a person not a place. Motorola's alleged vision of a world where every child gets a name and a phone number at birth is not that far off. My niece's four-week-old daughter already has an e-mail address and will have her own phone number too, as soon as she can talk.

Now that those phones can send and receive e-mails or surf the web while we walk down the street, who knows, or needs to know, where anyone is anymore? But how can you control people if you can't know where they are or what they are doing? Offices used to be some sort of corrals for people who had sold their time to the organization, but now the horses are all loose and there may not be enough cowboys to herd them up when needed.

Schools won't, in theory, need to herd in their pupils every day, teaching them over the Internet instead, and one can imagine governments attracted by the sort of savings possible with virtual schools. They can carry all the textbooks they will ever need in one e-book with 150,000 pages of text. But not all teenagers are eager students of the Open University, self-disciplined and self-organizing. No longer will weary parents heave a sigh of relief when their kids are safely parked inside the school gates. Will we therefore see electronic tagging replacing the roll call in the schoolroom? And will that be a good thing?

Property, too, becomes baffling. In this new world, ideas, information and intelligence are the new sources of wealth. But this wealth is different. I can give you everything I know, but I still know it and still have it after I have given it to you, unlike land or cash. Intelligence, likewise, is hard to pin down or stake. We can't dish it out or redistribute it, nor can we tax it because what can't be measured can't be taxed. Sometimes we want everyone to know our ideas, but sometimes we want to keep them to ourselves, but how do you patent ideas unless they take on a visible shape and form?

Increasingly, therefore, it is going to be harder to own what we produce, something that will give lawyers a lot of fun and doubtless much profit. Access rather than ownership will be what matters, and in some ways a world of unowned property might boost economies because it will allow those who own nothing to join in. American law has recently made it possible to patent genes. Firms or organizations holding those patents can then charge a fee to anyone wants to use those genes for research or to develop new treatments. They will be charging for access to knowledge that they claim they discovered. If this law is upheld it will blur the distinction between discovery and invention. The genes weren't invented; they were always there, just not isolated or named.

Hitherto patents were only granted to inventions. Luckily the first persons who stumbled on the tea plant never thought of patenting the leaf. Had this been done arguably there would be far fewer tea drinkers in the world today, because all tea growers would have had to pay a royalty. If it turns out that it is possible to lay claim to newly discovered bits of nature, be they genes or flora, that vision of a world of unowned property will be doomed. Some will get rich but the world as a whole will be poorer.

Some hope that an almost-free world of information and knowledge will bring equality of opportunity to all and that we must not put that possibility at risk by charging for access. The liberals' dream could come true, or be killed for ever, depending on how we treat knowledge as property. Keep knowledge free and villagers in India could have access to the world outside just as easily as the rich man in his Californian hideaway. Monopolies break down when anyone can access the purchasing hubs set up by the corporate coalitions such as the automobile companies, putting their products alongside the big boys for comparison. Knowledge can rain down upon the poor and the wealthy, the near and the far, alike. Education for all becomes a real possibility.

Others, however, fear that this new resource of information will, like all the sources of wealth that have gone before, sort out the rich from the poor. Even if the new knowledge is free, only the rich organizations can afford to buy those portals which are the entry to the web, so that when, two years ago, I wanted to find some financial information on Netscape I was first confronted with the array of Citibank's products. Being lazy I was tempted to look no further. And they say that Citibank paid $40 million at that time to get this jump start on their competitors.

Some experts think that, before long, 80 per cent of online commerce will be done by just thirty companies. The rich will have hogged it all. It is simply that the new rich may be different from the old rich, as has always happened in revolutions be they of arms or of technology. In which case we shall have to wait a generation or two, no doubt, before the new rich begin to take on the lessons of *noblesse oblige*, or rather *richesse oblige*, and start to do what they can to help the new poor.

There are those, too, who fear that putting our records, our words and our finances into cyberspace will destroy the whole concept of the right to privacy. If you want to keep any information to yourself you will have to hide it behind an armour of encryption, expensive and complicated for ordinary mortals. Conversely, others fear that, behind this same armour, all sorts of unholy alliances could flower undetected.

Even without encryption unlikely alliances may spring up out of nowhere. In the late summer of 2000 one of those unlikely alliances, of truckers and farmers, brought Britain to a halt in three days by blockading the oil terminals. The government could find no organization with which to negotiate and were stymied. The protests in Seattle against the World Trade Organization and globalization earlier that year were also planned and fanned over the Internet as an alliance with no apparent centre. Does this mean that democracy is moving out of parliaments and congresses and onto the Internet and the streets? If so, it will make government even more difficult than it already is. Politicians will have to deal with networks of fleas rather than the unionized elephants of old who may have been obstinate but at least you knew who they were and where they were.

The new e-world is therefore a mixed blessing. Much will get quicker and often cheaper, with, however, some unexpected side-effects. But manna from heaven can't be returned just because it doesn't fall equally or because you don't like the taste. We shall have to learn to embrace the inevitable, not ignore it, nor be overly enamoured of it. In the end we shall adapt, as humans always have, and in the end, too, life, love and laughter will continue, even if the paraphernalia is more exotic and more digital than we have been used to. Spring will still smell as nice, perhaps nicer since information does less harm to our environment than messy steel or cars, and Shakespeare's plays will still have resonance because they deal with love and jealousy, ambition and avarice, pride and compassion, death and the meaning of life, and such things do not go away.

THE REALLY NEW ECONOMY

It is as easy to dismiss the new technology as superficial as it is to be seduced by what it seems to promise. The truth is in between. Many types of work will continue as they have always done, albeit computer-enhanced, but some will go, never to return, and many new ones will be invented. Town planners, architects and designers may use computers to turn their ideas into working models that they can walk through and round on screen, but there will still be town planners, architects and designers in twenty years' time even if we call them by more grandiose names by then. 'I was trained as an architect,' a young woman told me, 'but now I call myself a space therapist.'

More importantly, we have been given a whole new way of communicating, of obtaining and exchanging information of all sorts, and are only at the beginning of the long string of possible effects which will significantly change the way we work. In that sense, the Internet may yet live up to the hype and turn out to be one of those 'disruptive technologies' that change the world for ever. The first of those changes is already appearing: the re-arrangement of whole industries, with often catastrophic consequences for the organizations involved. Bad news for one organization is often, however, a good opportunity for another. Creativity is born out of chaos, even if it is sometimes difficult to glimpse the possibilities in the midst of the confusion.

The middles of whole industries are disappearing. The industry in which I am most closely involved, publishing, is one example. At present there is a long chain of processes and organizations between me, the author, and you, the reader. There is also, usually, the author's agent and then the publisher. The publisher in turn, once the book is edited, employs a designer and a printer to produce a finished article. The finished book then goes to the warehouse of a distributor or a wholesaler and thence on to a bookstore, where, hopefully, someone will buy it and read it.

Everything in that chain of distribution is now in doubt apart from the beginning and the end, the author and the reader, but how the first connects with the second is now open to a wide range of options. We could dispense with the physical bookstore, the option focused on by Amazon.com and its imitators. The publisher could choose to bypass wholesalers and bookstores, virtual or physical, and publish electronically.

Or, if I was intrepid enough, as the author I could bypass the lot of them and put my words on a website for anyone to download for a fee. Taking it a step further, there is then nothing to stop someone adding his or her comments to it and passing it on, rather as medieval manuscripts were annotated as they circulated or, in the hi-tech world, in the way that the computer system Linux has been developed. Who then owns the resulting book? Or will it have to be free, as Linux is, for anyone to use it if they wish? And how then will I get paid?

It is given the wonderful name of disintermediation, this

phenomenon of disappearing middles in whole industries which allows newcomers to insert themselves into the gaps. When something acquires such a technical soubriquet you can at least be sure that it is happening. Any information business is now prone to a disappearing middle. Travel agents, the intermediaries between the traveller and the travel companies, are unnecessary now that you can obtain all the information that they have by clicking a few keys yourself. Newspapers and news bulletins may not be needed, are already not used by many in America, when you can get the news, packaged as you would like, more immediately, on your own screen, even on your mobile phone.

The whole television industry is about to experience disintermediation with the arrival of two hundred or more channels to choose from and the PVR or Personal Video Recorder that will one day be able to record hundreds of hours of your favourite programmes and then replay them at a time of your choice with or without the ads. Tony Garland of Universal Studios Networks has called it 'appointment viewing'. It means, for instance, that the channels may effectively have to pay you to watch the ads, charging you, say, £2 for a film without the ads but only 50p for one with the ads included – an upside-down world that some in the industry will find it hard to get their heads around.

They won't be alone in that. One problem for the elephants will be how to react quickly enough to a world that is so radically different from the one they have grown used to and been successful in. It is hard to abandon the habits of a lifetime when those habits have served you so well. Every business will have to re-examine its underlying business idea to see if it is still relevant, if they can still make money the way that they used to.

The music industry is another example. It fears that its CDs, which form the middle between the recording studio and the listener, will no longer be bought now that anyone can download their favourites from the Internet via Gnuttella or one of its successors for free, swapping their recordings directly with unseen friends. The process now has a generic name P2P, or peer-to-peer.

P2P is yet another of those disruptive technologies that could rip the heart of still more industries. The Free World Dial-Up project links private telephones across the world. You dial locally, the system routes the call via the Internet to the other country where someone else's private phone makes another local call to the number you want. You will have made an international call for the price of two local ones, both of which could, in certain countries, be free. How, then, will telecom companies make their money?

The disappearing middles continue. Stockbrokers aren't needed any more now that you can buy and sell your own shares directly from your computer or your phone. Auction rooms will go the way of stock exchanges, moving on to the screen. Maybe even doctors will become unnecessary if we find it easier to describe our symptoms to an anonymous website and get back an authoritative diagnosis that would allow us to obtain prescribed medicines or hospital appointments.

Politicians will find that national parliaments get squeezed out between more powerful local assemblies and the growing importance of regional economic blocs. They will squeal loudly about the loss of national sovereignty as it happens but disintermediation is one of those unintended but inevitable consequences of the way the new technologies push everything to be more local as well as more global, losing the middle in the process.

The most intriguing, and important, disappearing middle may well be the banking system. Smart cards are on their way to creating a form of private money. Many companies operate credit schemes cheaper and better than banks. Ford, it is sometimes said, is really a bank masquerading behind automobiles, a product that it might be tempted, at times, to use as a loss leader. Private clearing systems, some of them already in existence, would, as David Howell points out in his book *The Edge of Now*, remove the need for central banks to hold reserves in order to settle interbank transactions. Economics out of control? Perhaps they already are, with the amount of money traded every day in London's financial markets being thirty times more than the country's total output of goods and services in a year, making a nonsense of any attempt by the central bank to control the exchange rate. Will these central banks have any function in future other than to hold a periodical meeting to decide the level of interest rates?

Thinking radically, almost everyone could be thought of as an intermediary between the source and the ultimate customer. Almost every job could be part of a disappearing middle in the next twenty years. With all the information in the world at your fingertips there is no limit to the possibilities of computer-aided Do-It-Yourself. Buy your car on the web, sell your old one at one of the auction sites, no need to visit a dealer. Why, then, will we need dealers at all?

The reason is that information without interpretation is only data. To turn it into knowledge that is useful requires analysis, an understanding of the context, and a technical awareness of the field in question. That takes time and energy. Most of us will have neither the time nor the inclination to educate ourselves in most of life's arenas. The middles of many industries, therefore, will still be needed, but in a new form. The delivery organizations will be replaced by a variety of guides, interpreters and teachers – individuals or small firms, mostly operating electronically, adapting the wealth of data to your needs. The work will still be there, in the middles, but it will be different, and, if past history is any guide, done by different people and organizations.

More broadly, the disappearing middles in traditional industries will open up opportunities to fill those spaces in new ways. Most of the current inhabitants of the traditional industries, however, are unlikely to respond quickly enough to the changes ahead, which will leave large gaps for newcomers to move into. That is because you have to stand outside the box to see how the box can be redesigned. As often as not, the newcomers who fill the gaps will come from outside the industry and be unnoticed by the incumbents until after they have arrived. Change comes down the bypass, outflanking the established players as they continue on their accustomed route.

The *Encylopaedia Britannica* management remained convinced that people would always want their collection of handsomely bound volumes, costing several thousand pounds, displayed on shelves in their living rooms. They sat and watched their revenues fall as first the *Grolio Encyclopaedia* was published on CD-ROM for $385 and then, in 1993, Microsoft's *Encarta*, which also included multimedia, became available for $100. Within a year *Britannica* had collapsed and the business had been sold. It has since been resurrected by its new owners as a free online information service financed by ads, but the brand has been damaged. All this is obvious in hindsight or to outside observers, but hindsight is only of use to the writers of the obituaries. Elephants need fleas scratching their skins to help them see the obvious before it is too late.

Disappearing middles will occur in society, as well as business, as we adjust to the consequences of a world that is increasingly dematerialized and virtual. National boundaries will slowly erode, losing their importance, along with national parliaments, in a more virtual world. If I download something from my computer I have no idea what country it is coming from. What, then, is the meaning of the territorial rights clause in my publisher's contract? Hitler's *Mein Kampf* is banned in Germany but Germans can buy it from Amazon.com. In 2001 I may be one of the 40 per cent in Britain with a computer in my home, but long before the next twenty years are through we won't even be calling them computers. They will be just those screens hanging on the wall that we touch or perhaps just ask, verbally, for what we want. Much of the stuff that we will buy and sell will come through those screens, and who will be able to track it to count it?

As it is, some parts of my income are already dematerialized or virtual. They come in the form of 'rights' which publishers in other countries pay to reproduce my books. Unless I tell the Inland Revenue or HM Customs and Excise there is no way, as far as I can discover, that anyone could know about it. Because, sadly, they are rather small amounts I am happy to be honest and declare them all, but I can see that it might be tempting not to do so if they were significant. More and more our tax collectors will have to rely on the honesty of the citizenry to harvest the taxes on our income that are due.

Income tax has traditionally been the easiest tax to collect, being done with the help of the employing organizations who deduct it at source. As more and more work gets contracted out to the smaller organizations or to individuals working as independent contractors this free collecting agency will cease to be as useful. Countries like Italy have progressively moved from trying to tax invisible income to taxing the stuff that can be seen and counted and, which, preferably doesn't move, such as a house. But property taxes have their limits, and sales taxes such as VAT are regressive – they hurt the poor more than the rich – and inevitably they push up inflation, which hurts everyone.

Politicians are getting cleverer at finding new 'stealth taxes', the ones that no one notices at first, but they will have to get cleverer still, maybe by taxing those flows of money through the exchanges. But that will require international agreements to ensure that all countries use the same level playing field, as the jargon has it. More tax harmonization, in other words, between countries, is probably inevitable. Alternatively those politicians will have to find more ways to make paying taxes acceptable to us, possibly through hypothecation, an ugly word meaning that taxes are tied to certain uses. Income tax would be broken down into a health tax, an education tax, a police tax, a defence tax and so on. Governments hate hypothecation because it ties their hands and forces them to be more open about how they spend our money, but it may be the only way to extract money from us without an expensive and invasive use of electronic inspection of our money flows.

It is not my intention here to reinvent the taxation system. I am using its future dilemmas only to illustrate how much society as well as business will be individualized in the world that lies ahead. Increasingly we will be private fleas over whom the institutions of government bureaucracy will have less and less control. Without our voluntary co-operation society could begin to fall apart. We are, I believe, more likely to be prepared to contribute to the local than to the national, to the organizations and structures to which we feel we belong, than to bureaucracies that we don't understand for purposes over which we have no control. Democracy, in short, will have to get much more local if it is going to work. The nation state, given thirty years or so, may well be one of those disappearing middles.

Jobs have changed, too, as the organizations grapple with the consequences of those disappearing middles. The fact that already in Britain less than half the working population have full-time permanent jobs in organizations should alert us to the size of the changes that are occurring around us, even if they haven't yet hit us personally.

When I joined the Shell Group from university I was very relieved to have a job at all, let alone one with such a prestigious organization that covered the globe. I wrote to my parents, 'My life is solved.' I meant that Shell would thenceforth take charge of my training and development, place me in positions where I could do most good and learn best, take reasonable care of my financial needs and those of any future family, and generally plan my career for me. I probably should not have believed the whole of their recruitment brochure but that was definitely their intention. Everyone whom I met in Shell in those early years had been with the company for all of their working life and had no thought of going anywhere else. Looking back, I am now amazed that I was so willing, even eager, to hand over my life to an organization, having only met a few of its people, and those not the most important.

The sort of organizational career that Shell then provided has changed beyond recall. Organizations no longer offer it, individuals neither expect nor want it. In the post-industrial societies work is hurriedly being reinvented. 'Employability' means 'think like an independent' and is understood as such by many of their staff. 'Flexibility' means that no one can guarantee anything for long. Loyalty these days is first to oneself and one's future, secondly to one's team or project and only lastly to the organization. Those who work with the elephants nowadays think of themselves as the new professionals, akin to the architects and lawyers and teachers of the old professions with career possibilities that reach beyond the organization where they currently happen to be working. 'Cosmopolitans' not 'locals', a sociologist would call them. The new enthusiasm, in Europe now as well as America, for MBA degrees, although of varying types and quality, plays to this new definition of business and management as quasi-professions.

The new jobs, moreover, even the fewer longer-lasting ones with the big organizations, will not guarantee the kind of retirement that our parents enjoyed. The new careers, where they still exist, are already shorter. In France, for instance, only 38 per cent of men between the ages of fifty-five and sixty-four are in paid employment, and the figures are coming down to that level all over Europe. Proper jobs will end for most at fifty-five, when with luck they will have another thirty years left to live. No pension scheme, state or private, is currently able to provide a comfortable living for those extra years. The hard, or maybe the good, truth is that we shall have to go on working after the proper job ends, but it will be bits and pieces of work, collections or 'portfolios' of work rather than the continuation of any proper job. The work will help to keep us healthy, useful and off the backs of the generation behind us who will be ill able to finance our so-called retirement, a word that itself may one day be extinct.

Paradoxically, however, businesses are now worried that life outside the organization is becoming so attractive to free and independent spirits that there is a real danger of losing their best and most innovative people. They didn't intend flexibility to go that far. The chairman of a big multinational said to me in private, 'What worries me is that I can't see why any ambitous young person would want to join my company, or stay there for long if they did join. My most important job is to change that as fast as I can.'

In order to keep their best actors on their books, business organizations have started to offer tempting developmental opportunities that go beyond the immediate needs of the job. They recognize, for example, that sabbatical intervals are what some of their most talented people want. Two of our friends, recently married, both in high-powered jobs with demanding organizations, decided that they wanted to use the first year of their marriage to travel the world. They were going to sell their new apartment, they told me, leave their jobs and take off, with no plans and an open-dated around the world ticket.

'You're brave,' I commented, 'leaving your jobs at this stage in your career.'

'Oh, that's all right,' they told me. 'Both our organizations have promised to take us back with no loss of seniority when we return.'

Life will be more chunky in future. Intense and demanding projects will alternate with the equivalent of sabbaticals, some paid for by an organization, some self-funded. In the early years of the sabbatical Sloan programme at the London Business School the average intake of twenty individuals were all paid for by their organizations. The programme is now more than twice the size and five times more expensive but over half of each group now pays for themselves. The first programme was all male. The mix is now more often one third women to two thirds men, not yet equal but nearer. Rightly so, as the lives of men and women are gradually becoming more alike, with a lot of work in the information and service world appealing to women, and more men with the time to attend to child care or cooking, whether they want to or not.

To add to the turbulence, mobile phones, computers and the Internet are changing not only how we work but where. As a result, organizations are now debating who actually needs a permanent room in an office, which is, they are uncomfortably aware, a capital asset available for 168 hours a week but often used only for twelve or less, sometimes just for the collection of mail. Bill Gates has predicted that, by the year 2050, 50 per cent of the working population will be operating from home. Somewhat surprisingly to some, a survey in 2000 for Britain's Department of Employment discovered that 23 per cent of British workers already spent some of the week working at home and another 38 per cent would like to do so. Even more surprisingly, most of them thought that their employers would be happy for them to do so. The future of work may be nearer than we suspected and Bill Gates' prediction may well have come true long before 2050.

Expect, therefore, to see more of the new type of clubhouse offices rather than the heap of mini-apartments that we have been used to call our offices if we were lucky enough to have one. Clubs are places where only members and their guests are allowed in, where the rooms are defined by function (eating, meeting, reading etc.) and open to all rather than assigned to individuals. You can book a private room for a specific period or purpose but you cannot, in a clubhouse, put your name on the door, unless you are the secretary or site manager.

Members of the organization will use the clubhouse for meetings, for networking or for some forms of individual work, but they will not have a space to fill with their own personal effects – it is becoming too expensive. Increasingly, more people are living as teachers have always done, with the customers most of the day, with access to a clubroom but doing most of their preparation and reporting at home. The clubhouse office is the hub for a network, a network that will include independents as well as employees. No longer, in fact, will it be easy to distinguish who is permament and who temporary in any project team. All will be members of the club, for a while.

People may moan about the loss of personal space but can soon become accustomed to the new way of working. They learn to value the freedom and the escape from the need to be seen that is still part of the unspoken contract in many offices. As compensation for the loss of personal space we can expect organizations to invest in making the clubhouse attractive and comfortable, even luxurious, with good food, gyms and even overnight accommodation. That means that the architecture of business will gradually change and with it the skylines of our cities. Already many offices of yesterday, unneeded now, are being converted into apartments for inner-city dwellers.

Factories, of course, have not disappeared, but much of the repetitive work soon will, thanks to automation. In place of the assembly line, however, we now have the call centre and the

24-hour supermarket. Few would pretend that these offer either much fun or room for personal growth; they represent a means to an end, not a career, never the centre of anyone's life. Part-time or shift work is popular, therefore, because it leaves time for other interests. It is only one piece of a varied portfolio of activities. To the surprise of many men, surveys have consistently shown that part-time work is liked by women, for whom the job is not always the salient part of life.

At the other extreme we are seeing the rise of the independent entrepreneur or alchemist – people who hope to create something out of nothing. The First Tuesday network meetings of would-be entrepreneurs in some thirty cities around Europe were an early manifestation of the new ferment for starting one's own enterprise, which has stirred the enthusiasm of the twenty-somethings. The initial fervour was dampened by the crash of the early dotcoms but, in Britain, Chemistry, who developed the same idea of bringing together entrepreneurs and venture capitalists on a regular basis, has found that its meetings typically attract upwards of a hundred would-be and practising alchemists.

Where does this find us as we leave behind what has been the century of the employee? With a much more multi-hued canvas of work, with more choices for more people but also with more responsibility thrust upon us for making those choices. Work has indeed expanded to fill the space available, as Parkinson observed long ago, but it has done so in a surprising variety of ways, not all of them paid. The elephantine organizations of old are still around but they are much slimmer now, and they are surrounded by a multitude of fleas, smaller independent suppliers, sub-contractors, advisers, consultants and new start-ups. Look inside the organization, too, and you find that individuals are encouraged to take responsibility for their own futures, to develop their special competences and sell themselves to project and team leaders. In this sort of world it behoves one to think and act as an independent talent whether outside or inside the organization. In what seems, at first glance, to be the world of the elephants, the fleas, surprisingly, may be the winners.

In the third part of this book I will describe how I coped with becoming an independent after nearly thirty years in organizations of one sort or another. It is the sort of transition that almost everyone will be required to make in the more flexible world that we are entering. Schooled for life in institutions, as I was, they will find it a challenge to take reponsibility for their own careers. The best of them will relish the freedom and the opportunities, others will find life outside the organization to be tough and cruel. They will have to learn, as I had to, how to sell and price themselves, how to arrange their own learning and development and how to balance their lives. There are no schools for this as yet, only hard experience and the lessons from those who have gone before.

6

THE VARIETIES
OF CAPITALISM

I used to think that capitalism was a dirty word. That was until I
found myself earning my living as part of its system. Most of
us don't think of ourselves as capitalists, but if we are living and
working almost anywhere in the world today we have implicitly
accepted its underlying set of beliefs. As I look forward to the
future I cannot ignore the possible consequences of what has
become the real religion of the Western world, and increasingly
of the East as well.

Francis Fukuyama, the American social historian, once said
that every society would eventually end up with a combination
of liberal democracy and free market capitalism. He called this
The End Of History. His book was not a triumphalist thesis – he
wasn't all that excited by what would emerge at the end of the
day. Democratic governments, for one thing, would always want
to try and give the people what they wanted in order to be re-
elected, even if it was not what was best for their long-term
interests. He described the inhabitants of future societies as akin
to dogs lying on their backs in the sun waiting to be tickled.

Focus group politics we would call it today.

I do not share Fukuyama's sense of historical inevitability about either democracy or capitalism. The danger is that the flaws in the capitalist system may be its undoing, leaving us with something much worse. I used to worry that democracy would destroy capitalism, because of the inequalities that capitalism seems to produce, returning us to a dirigiste socialism or a dictatorship of the poor, but now I worry that capitalism may make political democracy redundant, as people find that the market gives them more power than a vote. In twenty years' time we should know which way it is going. My hope is that we can do something about the flaws in capitalism before then, although I am not optimistic.

My views on capitalism have been largely shaped by my experiences of three very different places – Singapore, America and Kerala in India – as well, of course, of Britain and Europe. Capitalism, I became aware, is not the same around the world. One question is whether the differences will remain or whether one brand of capitalism, the American one, will become so powerful that it will overwhelm the rest. If so, will it enrich the poor of the world or impoverish them even further? May it, perhaps, overwhelm us as individuals, distorting our values and priorities, or is it, as some would believe, the only path to freedom? Are liberty and equality ever reconcilable, or do we need the intervening fraternity – that French trinity of virtues that society still finds so elusive? I have lived and worked in a variety of capitalist cultures all my life but still have no clear answers to these crucial questions, yet if we do not find an answer the whole world of both elephants and fleas may come tumbling down.

SINGAPORE

I first encountered a very British form of capitalism forty-five years ago, in Singapore.

One day, during my first year working for Shell in Malaya, I received a message to report to the head office in Singapore. The General Manager wanted to see me. There was no indication, of course, of why. Organizations, then as now, cultivated an unnecessary aura of secrecy. When I got there, wondering what I had done wrong, he told me that London had asked them to appoint an economist for the region. 'I would like you to do this and to start straightaway,' he said.

'But I'm not an economist. I studied Latin and Greek.'

'But you got a degree, am I right?'

'Yes.'

'Well then, you'll be fine.'

And he showed me out.

I went downtown and bought a small yellow book called *Teach Yourself Economics* and started to read. A degree, I had just discovered, was not a qualification but a licence to learn. The very next week I was passed an invitation from Professor Parkinson, he of the famous Parkinson's Law, who was then teaching at Singapore's fledgling university, asking someone to come and talk to his seminar on the Future for Oil. 'You're the economist,' I was told, 'you do it.' I discovered something else then, that the best way to learn something is to try to teach it to someone else. It's bad luck on the students, I often think, but I have found it an excellent way to develop my thinking ever since.

The reason for the economist, I soon discovered, was that the Group office in London was beginning to get more professional in their forecasting. This was only 1956 and the days of guesswork, based on past trends, were only then coming to an end. They wanted estimates of GDP, meaning Gross Domestic Product my little yellow book told me, broken down by categories, from every region. Singapore, however, was still a crown colony. It had lots of statistics of people and their occupations, of goods produced and traded, but no one had ever put money numbers against them and tried to work out the total economic output. I would have to do it myself as best I could.

I don't imagine that I did it very well, but I learnt a lot about wealth and wealth creation. It was not, I realized, a subject that particularly interested Singapore's colonial administrators at that time. Administration, law and defence were their preoccupations. Strangely, it wasn't so different from the old communist regimes, I later reflected. What mattered most were planning and control, not enterprise or individual initiative.

Singapore was a well-run trading centre. Very little was actually made there; it was a city of servants and small shopkeepers. People were poor, apart from the expatriates. My forecasts did not anticipate much economic growth, and Singapore's best future seemed to lie in linking up with the newly-independent Malaysia. Wealth creation, it seemed to me, depended on investment, on a motivated and skilled workforce and on government expenditure on infrastructure, including higher education. The British weren't all that interested in these things.

I left Singapore in 1961. On my return thirty years later everyone on the flight was handed an introductory leaflet. The front page was a photograph of Orchard Road, Singapore's main street, looking just as I remembered it. Then I noticed the heading: 'Singapore – as it used to be'. Most of the world's cities, when you revisit them after thirty years, are still much as they were, with a few new buildings altering the skyline in places. I could not find my way around the new Singapore. All the old landmarks were gone, except for the cathedral and the cricket club, those enduring reminders of a colonial past. Singaporeans, I reflected, were now richer than the British, and their economy was growing faster. With a population the size of Ireland's or New Zealand's, and no natural resources, they had overtaken the British.

Singapore had initially joined Malaysia but soon left to stand alone, when the Chief Minister, Lee Kuan Yew, realized that his country would be dominated by the other states in the new federation. He records in his memoirs how he slept little on the night after he had announced independence, worried by what he had done. The little island had nothing, not even its own water, which still comes through a pipeline from the Malaysian mainland. He was staking his country's future on a belief in the capabilities of its people, in what we would now call their potential intellectual property.

His gamble, for that was what it was, was abundantly justified. Harry Lee, the Cambridge-educated radical lawyer, as he was when I first met him, had proved that capitalism can, in one generation, produce riches out of nothing, turning a Third World society into one able to compete with the First, even to top the league tables of that world in productivity.

That's what the statistics say. But is life necessarily better, I wondered? Much of Singapore seemed to be one extended shopping mall, filled with people selling, people buying. Much of that new GDP, I reflected, was *chindogu*, a word the Japanese use to describe the unnecessary things that we buy – windscreen wipers for your spectacles in the rain is one of my favourite examples. But *chindogu* also includes that extra pair of shoes that I don't need, the twenty ties hanging in my cupboard that I never wear, the books that I order from Amazon on impulse and never get around to reading, or all the expensive products of our son's bouts of retail therapy.

Chindogu is one of the first signs of capitalism's problem of excess. Economic growth requires more people to spend more money. That in turn provides more work for more people, creating more money to spend on more things, and so the spiral of growth continues. It is the sort of spiral that America enjoyed at the end of this last century and, give or take a few temporary lulls, it has been the story of the world economy over the last fifty years. That could hardly be called a problem.

It isn't, as long as there are ever more appetites to be satisfied. Capitalism falters if demand diminishes, when we move beyond our needs and can't be persuaded to want more than we have. A faltering consumer demand was Japan's problem in the Nineties, when the government even considered giving people vouchers to tempt them into the shops. New products and product upgrades titillate our appetites and keep demand alive. So does the desire to have what we see others having, or to have what they don't have. Fashion, boosted by advertising, is an important stimulus to demand, as is envy.

I was enough of an economist to recognize that *chindogu* has its uses in providing employment and more money for people to spend, but a part of me worried about the waste involved in all those unnecessary things, the waste of people's time as much as the waste of materials. It can't be much fun standing in those shopping malls all day and increasingly all night promoting *chindogu*, even if it is upmarket stuff, nor can it be satisfying to be one of those who produce it, in a factory or, nowadays, to be sitting in a call centre backing up yet another unneeded website. Not the best use of a life, I reflected, even if it does provide the bread to sustain that life.

A part of me worried, too, about a world where the rich were locked into the spiral of growth and increasing opulence, while more than four billion people throughout the world were still living in poverty, an imbalance that capitalism seems to be unable to correct, and may even be making worse. Singapore, however, had shown how capitalism could be harnessed to the advantage of the poor, given determined leadership. In thirty years it had managed to lift all its citizens out of poverty, only for some to find that their increasing aspirations are creating their own problems.

'It's odd,' a young Chinese banker there told me, 'my income is at least five times greater than what my father earned, but my parents had a house and garden, with a live-in servant and a car. Houses with gardens are rare now, and too expensive. I live in a fifth-floor apartment with no servant. I don't own a car because you have first to buy a permit which costs almost as much as the car. My father came home at six every evening. I don't get home until after nine most days. I don't really know who was truly richer, my father or myself.'

That's one other problem with successful capitalism: you have to swim twice as hard to stay in the same place. Two incomes and longer working days are needed to live as well, relatively, as one's parents did on one income. The word 'relatively' is important, because few would want to go back to the physical conditions in which our parents lived, for all the nostalgia about their slower and easier world. The reality is that we compare ourselves with those about us, not with our past or our parents. The river of affluence may be flowing fast and carrying us with it, but if we don't watch the bank and, instead, look only at the people alongside us we won't feel that we're moving at all.

Politicians continue to be disappointed when no one thanks them for economic growth, but they shouldn't be surprised. We aren't looking backwards as they are, proud of their record; we are comparing ourselves with our contemporaries. Furthermore, if economic growth puts more people into the swim, the river becomes more crowded, the conditions more stressful and more competitive. Some are then tempted, as I was, to leave the river, sit on the bank and watch the others struggle. But if everyone opted out in that way the economy would falter and they would soon be complaining that the roads were full of potholes, health care deteriorating and schools failing to educate their children. Those who sit on the bank are inevitably freeloading on the economic infrastructure that is financed by the wealth created by the swimmers.

I realized, as I walked the clean, safe streets of the new Singapore, that I had no answers to these problems. They were not, however, problems that greatly exercised the locals. Most of them seemed to like all the getting and spending. Even my friend who was comparing his lot with that of his parents was doing so ruefully, not angrily or even nostalgically. Singaporeans seem proud of their state and of what they have achieved.

Westerners acknowledge the economic achievements of Singapore but often deplore the supression of dissent, what they see as the control-freakery of its government and the docile conformity of its people. 'Would you like to live there now?' they ask. Well, I can reply, there is much to commend it for the foreigner who is not concerned with the politics of the place. Things work in Singapore. Drugs and violence are rare. It is well-regulated and well-policed. There is no detectable under-class. They do many sensible things, such as paying their civil servants and ministers good salaries, too good in some ways because they suck talent out of the private sector. Their pension arrangements are a model of self-provision, with everyone tucking away 30 per cent of their income in a provident fund against which they can borrow for things like mortgages. It is, most expatriates would agree, a good place in which to do business and house a young family.

To appreciate Singapore one has to discard the individualist assumptions of Anglo-American capitalism which is driven by the ambitions and needs of each individual. Lee Kuan Yew has proved that a different kind of capitalism can work in certain situations and cultures. He calls it a guided capitalism. I think of it more as corporate capitalism. Singapore is run much as one would run one of the corporate elephants, the assumption being that what is good for the corporation is good for all its inhabitants, the very reverse of the individualist tradition. Instead of the state being the servant of the indivdual, the individual is expected to be prepared to make some compromises for the good of the state. Singapore is not going to suit the independent-minded flea or alchemist.

That, in fact, as I have said, is one of their current concerns. They need more creativity to maintain their pattern of growth. Lee Kuan Yew, still the philosophical driving force of Singapore, has himself said that the time has probably come to relax the extent of the 'guiding' and to allow more individualist expression. It will be interesting to see whether the two traditions can merge successfully, or whether allowing the individualist assumptions to infiltrate will contaminate that carefully organized society.

America, I was to discover, was a very different place.

AMERICA

I was thirty-four years old when I first went to America, in 1966. It was then a rather mythical place for many. The days when holidays in Florida or California were common, or when executives thought little of flying to New York for a day's business, were still awaiting the arrival of cheap air fares. I was going to the Massachusetts Institute of Technology to learn the theories and practice of business in the land where, I gathered, business and the schools of business were universally admired.

It was different in Britain in 1966. There were no proper business schools, and business was not something thought worthy of serious study. When I told a friend that I was going to MIT in preparation for joining the new London Business School, he looked puzzled, then asked if MIT stood for the Montreal Institute of Typing. Back then, to most people in Britain, a business school meant a secretarial college.

I loved America, I loved the openness and friendliness of the people. I liked the fact that they weren't English, that they accepted you as you and not for what your parents were. I warmed to their infectious enthusiasms and even their strangely loud voices. But the start was inauspicious. I had been married for four years. We travelled with our new baby, only six weeks old. There had been a small outbreak of smallpox in continental Europe earlier that year, so we had taken the precaution of carrying a letter from our doctor explaining that the baby was too young to be vaccinated, just in case the immigration authorities asked questions. They did, and they weren't satisfied by the letter.

It was a very hot afternoon when we landed and the immigration officer was sweaty and tired. He had instructions, he said, to let in nobody from Europe who had not been vaccinated. We would have to go into quarantine for five weeks in an isolation ward of a hospital, at our expense. We argued, expostulated, pleaded. In the end he let us in provided I agreed to sign a document on behalf of MIT indemnifying the US government against any outcome of our possible infection, up to a maximum of $10 million. He knew, and I knew, that I had no authority to sign anything on behalf of MIT, but he had his bit of paper and we had our baby.

Later, I reflected that the encounter had told me a lot about the land I was entering. I was impressed that someone at the lower end of a big organization should have had the gumption and the authority to come up with such an innovative solution on his own initiative. He had not needed to consult his superiors at any stage. That sense of personal responsibility and initiative was something I was to encounter time and time again. It goes beyond the job. Americans seem to understand that their life is their own responsibility and no one else's. In a well-functioning society, they feel, where everyone takes on that responsibility, there should be no need for a welfare state. Britain's National Health Service, I was continually told, was a sign of a flabby society. How awful, they said, to have to trust your health to a bureaucracy that you could not influence.

I was also struck by the fact that money provided the solution to our immigration dilemma. I don't mean that the officer was influenced by money, rather that he looked to a financial way out. So much of what I was to meet in America came with dollar signs attached. How successful are you? means, often, what is your salary, what fees do you charge, or what is your net worth? Running for political office? You'll need to find a lot of money. You got hurt in an accident? Get someone to sue for financial compensation. You want to give something back to society? Endow a university professorship or an art gallery.

I learnt later that the Puritans, who landed in America shortly after the Pilgrim Fathers, brought with them the belief that money you had earned yourself was a sign of your worth as a human being, something to be proud of, not ashamed. Work was good, good work should rightly earn more than bad work, therefore more money means more good achievement. I'm not sure that the syllogism still holds, but the sense that money is not only useful but also nothing to be ashamed of is a deep-rooted part of American culture, bequeathed to them, oddly, by an ascetic group of English people.

Coming as I did from a world where money was something best not talked about, where thrift and a modest lifestyle were things to be proud of, where money might provide the means of life, but certainly not its meaning, America was profoundly shocking at first – and then wonderfully liberating.

It was exciting to feel that I need not be ashamed to use my talents to make money or to spend it how I liked. My financial success, if it came, would be proof that I was contributing as much good to the world as any more altruistic career. I would now retract some of that early fervour but I could see, at once, why Americans were such avid proponents of their pure capitalist world. It was a world that I was to find full of paradoxes and puzzles.

One week later I attended my first economics lecture. The professor started by stating the unambiguous and unchallenged purpose of any business: to optimize the medium-term return to shareholders. Money, I noted once again, was the measure, this time of business success. I felt then, and I feel now, that that was too simplistic. Most people, including myself, do not have the shareholders at the front of their mind while doing their jobs. Nor do I believe that they should.

Business, any business, has multiple objectives which include providing good value for its customers, offering a worthwhile job and opportunities for personal growth for its workers, investing in its future stream of products, respecting the needs of the local communities in which it operates and the environment in general, and, of course, making sure of a proper return for its financiers. It is naive to believe that these often conflicting objectives will all come together in one number called share-holder value. It is the peculiarly difficult job of top management to balance these objectives. Give too much priority to one of them and you risk defaulting on the others.

I once found myself sitting next to 'Chainsaw' Al Dunlap at a private seminar. Dunlap had acquired his nickname through his passion for ruthlessly getting rid of every cost and person not directly producing immediate added value to the bottom line of profits. When he declared that the only purpose of a company's existence was to return as much money as possible to its owners as soon as possible, I found myself exclaiming 'Nonsense!' in an unnaturally loud and very English-sounding voice. Giving me no chance to elaborate he turned on me, 'That's what's wrong with your country. Your business leaders don't understand what they are there for.' I was not surprised to hear, three years later, that Mr Dunlap had collapsed the company that he was supposed to be responsible for, having so decimated its staff that it lost its way to the future, and had himself lost his job.

I am still at a loss to understand why shareholders are given such priority in the Anglo-American version of capitalism. It is not as if they actually 'own' the company in any real sense. They haven't in most cases even provided it with money. The first shareholders of each business did indeed give the company money in return for its shares, but thereafter those shares changed hands through the various stock exchanges without any more money going to the company. The shareholders aren't financing the business, just betting on it. The stockmarket is a secondary market for the most part, at one remove from the actual business.

The price at which the shares are exchanged in that market does matter to the company, however, because if the price is high it allows the company to use its shares to buy other companies, or to raise new money, while if the price falls too far it leaves the company open to being bought by another. So when company chairmen talk so fondly of their shareholders, most of whom they have never met, they are really talking about their share price, which is affected by the profits and dividends they can declare and the sort of future they are thought to offer. Money, in the sense of the share price, does then become the real measure of success.

The share price is the corporate currency of capitalism, especially in its American version. Businesses use their shares to buy other businesses. It's the quickest way to grow the company, to fill in any gaps in the strategy, and, if one is cynical, to provide bigger jobs for those at the top. Research, however, consistently shows that some two thirds of mergers and acquisitions don't add value. The only people who benefit financially are those who owned shares in the company being purchased. What I find disturbing about the whole process is that businesses become commodities, things to be bought and sold, whether those who work there want it or not.

When I left my corporate home in Shell I worked for a year in an offshoot of Anglo-American, the South African mining company. Charter Consolidated, based in London, was intended to be a way for Anglo-American to relocate some of its assets outside South Africa. I was employed as an economist – that Singapore interlude had come in useful and allowed me to reclassify myself. At the end of my first week I was handed a bundle of company reports, all in French, along with a number of South African ones. 'Harry [Oppenheimer, the big chief in Johannesburg] wants to swap parts of the South African ones for the French ones. He wants to know if it's a fair deal.' I did my best; it was a nice intellectual challenge, and I was pleased with myself when I worked out that Harry stood to lose some £2 million by the deal. He'll be gratified to know that I have saved him that, I thought.

The next day one of Harry's lieutenants dropped by to see how I was getting on, before he went back to South Africa. I told him my worry about the two-million deficit on the deal.

'Oh, is that all?' he said. 'Harry will be pleased. It's a small price to pay for buying a stake in Europe.'

I realized that I had joined the world of corporate finance, where companies were just a means to an end. I had to confess that during all my calculations and projections I had not given a thought to the people who worked in those companies whose destinies I was helping to decide. I didn't even know the towns where they were located. It was sexy stuff, playing chess with companies, but there was too much power, surely, in my apprentice hands. The corporate chess players of New York's or London's investment banks are cleverer at it than I could ever have been, but I doubt that they give any more thought to the people they are buying and selling than I did.

The share price, moreover, is a fickle mistress. Its ups and downs owe as much to the fads of the moment as to the actual performance of the business, allowing some trendy new economy stocks, for instance, to achieve a high share price in spite of never having declared a profit. The stockmarket itself is also subject to its own mix of supply and demand. More money chasing the same number of shares will push most prices up, whether they deserve it or not. While if the demand for shares falters, perhaps because of some political uncertainty or fears of recession, then prices will fall irrespective of how well an individual firm may be performing. A rising stockmarket in the Nineties tempted many Americans to borrow in order to buy some of those rising shares, thus boosting the demand and pushing the market higher. If the US government decides, as one day it may, to part privatize their underfunded social security, some $100 billion of tax revenues will flow into the market each year, pumping it ever higher. The reverse, however, could also happen if too many ordinary citizens got worried and decided to try to sell their shares.

It seems illogical, even bizarre, to use such a casino as the basis for a whole society's system of wealth creation. The odd thing is that it works, or has done thus far, more or less continually in America since the Second World War. Individuals become multimillionaires by taking their businesses public. Executives are rewarded for achievement with options to buy their company's stock at favourable prices. Individuals borrow money to invest in the stockmarket casino. The possibility of riches beyond mere salaries inspires individuals to take their dreams to market, to start businesses, build them bigger, or make them more productive. The pursuit of personal riches is still the engine that drives the American capitalist machine. Those riches give enterprising individuals the freedom to live life as they want, to buy the choices that the market offers.

The other odd thing is that, at the top end, this is not money for spending. No one, no matter how profligate, could spend the tens of millions of dollars that the richest Americans take home each year as the fruits of their labours. In 1999 there were 268 billionaires on the *Forbes 400* list of the richest Americans and you had to have $625 million just to get onto the list. This is money as an object in itself, money as a prize. Often the super rich will hug their prizes to themselves, taking private satisfaction from their success, dressing down, avoiding signs of opulence. Stealth wealth, they call it. Some like to go more public. Where the British award knighthoods and baronies as signals of achievement, Americans buy their own awards. Some flaunt their vineyards and yachts, others put their names on foundations or museums, using their prize money to reward themselves with the distinctions that they feel their work has earned. I'm not sure that I don't prefer the American way.

But, as always, there is a snag. Most Americans do actually need the money not as a prize but to spend, because most of them don't have enough of it. When they look at the money the top people take home and compare it with their own earnings they must wonder at a system that can reward the top managers in a company five hundred times more than the average worker in that business. We are not talking about the individual talents of sports stars like Michael Jordan or of entrepreneurs like Bill Gates, but of more ordinary salaried executives. How, ordinary people wonder, can any one individual's work be valued at five hundred times that of another when they both work for the same organization? Can one person have made that much more difference?

The statistics reveal that the bulk of Americans have not seen their real earnings increase significantly during America's boom years. Eighty-six per cent of the stockmarket gains of the Nineties went to only 10 per cent of the population, leaving most of the rest unaffected. The Federal Reserve found that although the median family net worth rose by 17.6 per cent between 1995 and 1998, family wealth was still 'substantially below' 1989 levels for all income groups under the age of fifty-five. In other words two people now work to maintain the relative standard of living that one of their parents probably achieved on their own. Statistically, America is now the most unequal society in the world, after Nigeria. America seems to be proof of the theory that the faster an economy grows, the greater is the gap between rich and poor, because the poor get left behind in a race where knowledge and skills count so much more than mere muscle.

It would seem, on the face of it, to be a situation waiting for socialism, but no socialist party in America has ever polled more than 8 per cent of votes in any election. Both the main political parties are committed to a capitalist society. The poor in America are really poor, but they are not rising in revolt, nor do the middle classes seem to feel that they are losing out, although statistically they are. As I wander periodically through America's downtrodden city centres and then its manicured and often gated suburbs, I wonder why this growing inequality, the thing that I imagined would be the Achilles' heel of capitalism, bringing it to an inglorious end, was not the worry for most of the poorest that I felt convinced it would be.

The answer, I believe, is unique to America. It goes back to those early Puritans and their emphasis on salvation through individual effort. It was bad Christian theology, no doubt, since it leaves no room for the idea of God's Grace, but they were Christians of an unusual sort. Our life, they taught, is our own responsibility, we cannot blame anyone else for our condition. The Puritans also believed that it was man's duty to create heaven on earth. Their leader urged them to build a model society, 'a city set on a hill'. Our purpose on this earth, they felt, was to improve on God's creation.

The idea that the future can and should be better than the past is one of the most invigorating aspects of American culture, so unlike the often weary European feeling that things can only decline from the golden days of the past. Add to this the immigrant culture with its tradition of building a new life in a new land and one can begin to understand why so many think that they, too, can one day share in the prosperity that they see around them. The envy that can be corrosive in other capitalist societies seems in America to fuel ambition and hope. This is reinforced by the churning that goes on at the bottom of the ladder. Over half of those at that level of the occupational grades have moved up one or two places in the past year, while others have moved down.

This movement suggests to those near the bottom that there is always possibility, always hope. It is, however, hope tinged with fear, because there is not much of a safety net for those who fail. Perhaps, I reflected, it is this very mix of possibility and fear that feeds the energy that is so palpable in America. If the mix changed, however, if the fear exceeded the possibility, as it did in the depression years, then the American mode of capitalism would be under threat. It is a tricky balance for the political leaders of the country to maintain.

Americans, it has always seemed to me, put their faith in the market, rather than in politicians, as their best chance to improve their lot. A book that came out in 2000, entitled *One Market Under God*, by the American commentator Thomas Frank, worried that nowadays markets 'express the popular will more articulately and meaningfully than do mere elections'. If that is so, then the poor are effectively disenfranchising themselves, yet don't seem to mind. Politics only becomes a concern to a lot of Americans when their governments start spending their money on foreign adventures. Domestic problems are more quickly solved at an individual level, by effort and money. Why vote, when it seldom seems to change very much? Hence the paradox that in this, the world's leading democracy, half of the population don't go to the polls. Capitalism is eroding democracy.

Does it matter? I think it does. It breeds a selfish society, a look-after-yourself-and-your-family society, a land of clubs and ghettos. Checking into a five-star hotel on one of my later visits – paid for, I'm pleased to say, by someone else's business – I found that the elevator would not stop at my floor. I complained to the reception desk. 'Oh, I'm so sorry,' she said, 'I forgot to give you the key to the club floor. Put this in the keyhole in the elevator and then press the button for your floor.' Privilege without responsibility. Very pleasant, too, with complimentary cocktails and snacks, and breakfasts up in the sky, away from the rest of the guests down in the basement.

It was, I thought, a parable of parts of modern America. Where everyone is insulated among their own kind, there is little contact with those down below and less concern for their lives. Politicians when campaigning don't talk too much about the very pressing problems that plague America with nearly two million people in their gaols, the drugs and guns in the streets and often in the schools, the increasing pollution of the environment and the racial tensions that still exist. They talk instead of what they can do for you, you the individual, not you the member of a community.

I'm not alone in feeling that capitalism is eroding much of the fellow feeling that used to distinguish American communities. Some distinguished Americans feel the same. Political scientist Robert Putnam's evocatively titled book *Bowling Alone* argues that Americans have seen a collapse in honesty and trust, that the system of social capitalism, where citizens benefit from shared networks and reliance on one another, is in crisis because of the rise of a crude individualism and the go-it-alone society. The market system, Adam Smith always argued, depended on what he called sympathy, the need to take care of your neighbour and to share your gains with those less fortunate. Erode that sympathy, and you risk destroying the basis of trust on which the dealings of the market ultimately depend.

Another distinguished American, Nobel prizewinner Robert Fogel, is worried by what he sees as a spiritual deprivation in America, largely as a result of capitalism's material success. He does not, however, mean a lack of spiritual faith but a dearth of such qualities as self-esteem, sense of family, a sense of discipline, an appreciation of quality, and – most important of all, he thinks – a sense of purpose. Once people have enough to eat, he argues, these qualities start to matter more than yet more material wealth.

Economic historian David Landes, in his magisterial work *The Wealth and Poverty of Nations*, goes further. He believes that the spirit of optimism no longer rings true. To many the future looks worse than the past; fanaticism, factionalism, and resentment are on the increase. He quotes Yeats: 'The best lack all conviction, while the worst/Are full of passionate intensity.'

I pick up some of David Landes' fears when I revisit America today, over a quarter of a century since my first arrival. It is still an exuberant, buoyant, energetic land, where I go to have my sense of the possible restored. But I do sense some of the selfishness concealed behind the exuberance. It is perhaps natural to be concerned first for oneself, given the insecurity that I also detect behind the bonhomie. Worried days have now hit the salaried middle classes who have lost the old security of the job but have not benefited from the winner-take-all world of the talented and the entrepreneur.

I also can't help but question why the United States need to employ 70 per cent of all the lawyers in the world and wonder whether that isn't the very visible sign of Robert Putnam's feeling of a collapse of trust. One friend, recently arrived from Britain with her young family, complained that her kids' friends never came to play.

'Why not?' we asked.

'Because they might hurt themselves, and their parents know that we don't have proper insurance.'

We looked puzzled, so she explained, 'It means that they won't get anything if they sue us.'

What kind of world will it be, I wonder, where children aren't allowed to play together?

I also note, on recent visits, an echo of Robert Fogel's worry about a lack of purpose. It's the old dilemma that when you've got what you want you don't want what you've got anymore – one more paradox of success. Ironically, therefore, a society that makes it ever easier for many to get what they want quite early in life, is laying itself open to an epidemic of ennui later on among many of its movers and shakers. Money buys many things in a capitalist system, but it does not, in the end, provide most of us with an adequate reason for our lives, once our material needs have been satisfied. There is, of course, always more *chindogu* to buy, but even this palls after a while. A worthwhile life, in my book, requires you to have a purpose beyond yourself, something that selfish capitalism puts low down on the agenda.

I always leave America energized and excited. But I also know that I don't want to live there. Their form of capitalism is too exhausting. Life becomes a long-distance race that you cannot afford to quit, but also one that you can never win, because there is always someone ahead, always more to get, more ways to do better or go faster. I have strong-minded friends there who define their own race, set their own pace and targets, but they are the minority and I would not, I suspect, be as strong as them if I lived there.

Is it possible to have a less demanding form of capitalism, I wondered? I needed to find out.

KERALA

Free market capitalism works in America – sort of. It has generated a huge amount of wealth and continues to do so. It is the distribution that is distinctly patchy. Americans, however, have always emphasized liberty more than equality, taking equality to mean equality of opportunity not equality of outcome. The third member of that virtuous trinity – fraternity – is also under threat, having become a matter of clubs for the rich and ghettos for the poor, rather than the mechanism for social cohesion that it needs to be.

Americans are evangelists for their country. They believe that what works for them should work everywhere. I wanted to test this assumption. It clearly did not work at first in Russia where it became an excuse for criminal syndicalism, a Mafia capitalism. Without the laws and institutions that keep markets under control, individualist capitalism can tear a country apart. Life expectancy for males in Russia declined by ten years in one decade. Pensioners are said to be living on the equivalent of $10 a month. Much of the country has returned to a state of subsistence agriculture. Things are slowly getting better and Russia may eventually create its own variety of capitalism, but it will take at least one generation to take root.

China, forewarned by what happened in Russia, is proceeding more cautiously. They recognize that they cannot resist the appeal of consumerism and the need to allow more commercial freedom but, for the sake of social cohesion, they are determined to preserve the structures of the communist state. They hope, I sensed on my visits there, that they will be able to evolve a particularly Chinese self-contained version of capitalism, recognizing that their home market will provide all the potential demand that they need without having, necessarily, to expose themselves to the global market. The other Asian economies, frightened by the collapse of its currencies in 1997–8, are paying more heed to strengthening their regulations and institutions in order to insulate themselves, if they can, from the vagaries of that market.

Europe, battered by two horrific wars in forty years, has traditionally been more concerned to emphasize a fair distribution and social cohesion than to go flat out for the generation of wealth. In Britain, during the Eighties, Margaret Thatcher set out to change the emphasis. She tackled the forces of resistance head on, facing down the trade unions, and happily watched the demise of many of the less efficient industrial elephants. In their place she sought to create an American culture of individual enterprise rewarded by financial gain.

It was a necessary change. The *status quo ante* was leading into a morass. But the price was high. 'There is no such thing as society, only individuals and families,' she famously said, meaning, quite reasonably in my view, that we had to take responsibility for our own lives. The outcry that greeted her words, however, was a sign of the hurt that many felt she had dealt to Britain's social cohesion. Inequality had grown, insecurity was widespread, the word 'underclass' had become part of the language, careers as we had known them had evaporated. Profit and financial reward became the indicators of success as state enterprises were sold off and taxes lowered.

Things did begin to work better but a new and ugly selfishness had been born. In due course the people voted for what they hoped would be a softer form of capitalism. They are still hoping. Once the genie of individualist capitalism is out of the bottle it is hard to put it back in. Lionel Jospin, the Prime Minister of France at the turn of the century, put the European view very nicely when he said that he wanted a market economy but not a market society. As he knows, that is easier to say than to achieve, but France is not alone in Europe in wanting to shield its people from the brutalities of American capitalism, even at the expense of a degree of growth.

Europe will, I hope, find its own softer version of American capitalism, but I wanted to see what effects the spread of global capitalism was having on the less comfortable parts of the globe, on the developing economies of the Third World. Was it raping them, as some observers suggested, exploiting their cheap labour, or was it bringing people the technologies and the means to lift themselves out of poverty? The statistics were not good. Whereas the richest 20 per cent of the world had 70 per cent of the wealth in 1960, this had risen to 85 per cent by 1990 and is probably higher still now. A billion people are living on less than a dollar a day. Does global capitalism have anything to offer them?

I decided to go to one of the more hopeful areas, to India, a huge country that miraculously still remains a democracy. I have been there many times. It seems to be a family tradition. Two of my mother's uncles were officers in the old Indian Army with exotic tales to tell of life between the wars. My mother's sister was a dedicated doctor, working in a mission hospital in Hazaribagh in Bihar, the poorest and roughest state in India. I visited her there once, and drove out with her in her huge old Chevrolet truck to her surgeries in the villages, where she was treated as a visiting angel, for she was the only sort of health care that they ever saw.

I was left in awe at the size of the country's problems, the endless flow of people, the lack of infrastructure, of even the basics of life. I was also humbled by the friendliness of the people and their quiet acceptance of what life had offered them. I remember, on one visit, seeing a woman standing by the road waiting for a bus as we drove by one morning. When we returned that afternoon she was still waiting, undaunted it seemed. The bus would come, eventually. I admired her patience, but such quiet acceptance did not, I felt, augur well for an enterprise society.

India was a socialist society back then, forty years ago. It has steadily become more capitalist. How, I wondered, would capitalism work in India, such a very different place to America.

As the new century started I was handed the opportunity to

find out, in an unlikely part of India. I was invited by the BBC to make three short radio programmes on Kerala, supposedly a model for enlightened development in the Third World, as well as a tourist paradise. I am not a very good tourist. Historic sights bore me, and an hour on a beach is long enough. People and their lives are much more interesting and I discovered some time ago that if you are carrying a tape recorder with the magic letters BBC on it, it is surprising how ready people are to talk with you.

Kerala is one of India's smallest states, although even that means a population of thirty million, gathered between the hills and the sea in the bottom western edge of that vast sub-continent. It is a lush green state, unlike the dusty brown of much of India, with rivers and inland waterways weaving their way down to the sea from the tea gardens in the hills to the rice fields and the beaches. Kerala is beautiful. It is also noteworthy for having had an elected communist government back in the Fifties, and communists are still partners in the ruling coalition today.

That early communist government began the slow-burn development strategy which is now seeing its first fruits. 'Hastening slowly' they called it, when setting out those early development plans. Hastening slowly meant building the foundations first, primary health care and primary education with particular emphasis on literacy and a focus especially on women. The results have been dramatic. Kerala has the lowest birthrate in India, only just above the replacement rate of 2.2 children per woman, and a literacy rate of 94 per cent in their own language of Malayalam. That is better than Britain and many countries in the First World.

The people are clever as well as charming. They can work out where their advantage lies, and, mostly, they can see that it doesn't lie in Kerala. The young of Kerala know about the global economy. The better skilled are working in Bombay or Delhi or even further afield, in California, Munich and London; the less skilled are providing the labour in the oil rich states of the Middle East, returning home every few years and retiring home for good in their fifties.

That is Kerala's problem with a global world. Educate your young and you lose them. The people who remain behind are well off by Indian standards, but the money comes from overseas relatives or from tourists. Both sources are contaminating. The state has attracted the hippy cavalcade, slipping down from overcrowded Goa to Kerala's long and empty beaches. I met young people on the famed Kovalam beach who reckoned they could live on £2 a day. Low-grade lodgings and eating houses jostle each other beside ramshackle Internet cafes behind the beach.

Kerala would like to see more upmarket tourism, more integrated into the life of its people, but the authorities find it is hard to stop the supply of tawdry offerings when the demand is there. Low-grade tourism cheapens a country even while it enriches some. It carries drugs, litter and commercial sex in its train, degrading both hosts and guests. This, I reflected, is one aspect of globalization that often isn't emphasized – the new mobility of the young, who can go anywhere in the world for the price of a rail ticket from London to Glasgow, often bringing with them the worst aspects of their home countries.

Remittances are another facet of this worldwide mobility. Because Kerala people are as globally-minded as the tourists, a lot of Kerala lives on the small change from their relatives who work all around the world (the main daily newspaper in the state prints one million copies a day, but sends one hundred thousand of them abroad). As a result there is money to spend in Kerala, much of it spent by the parents and wives of those left behind. They spend it, naturally enough, on the consumer goods that the First World takes for granted, on television sets, washing machines and computers. Then they want a modern brick house to keep them in and a car to ferry themselves around.

The new spending crowds the inadequate roads and draws people into the towns where there is no room for them and no jobs. More significantly none of what they buy comes from Kerala, apart from the bricks and labour for their new houses. The remittances don't generate new work, only new imports. To pay for those imports Kerala exports its people, often the best of its people.

'We are the Irish of India,' one man told me.

'But the Irish are coming home to Ireland,' I said. 'When will your people come back to Kerala?'

I spoke with several young Kerala executives who worked in Bombay. Yes, they said, Kerala was a lovely place and they loved coming back to see their families but they wouldn't live there.

'Why not?'

'Because there aren't any jobs for us there. There's no excitement, nothing to do.'

It was the way I felt about Ireland when I was young. I left, too, and never went back, except to see my family.

Ireland's economy took off when one thousand American multinational firms located there, lured by the government's tax concessions, a well-educated young labour force and entry to the European market. On the back of that influx local enterprise began to establish itself, and the Irish came back. Kerala sits, like Ireland, on the edge of a huge market, and like Ireland probably needs an initial boost from overseas to get it moving. It needs a few magnet corporations who might become the core of the sort of clusters that generate alchemy and more enterprises. The state has created a brand-new technology park but there is no queue yet to occupy it.

Instead, the socialist coalition government has opted for land reform, redistributing the acres of padi fields from the rich landowners to the smallholders who used to work those fields. The intention is to give more people economic independence and to keep them on the land. But land reform is a pre-industrial remedy for a world that is now post-industrial. The new fields are too small to yield a profit, and people want more than subsistence farming. They want surplus cash to buy what they need. They want jobs, not land, they told me.

You might think, as I did, that Kerala was perfectly positioned for the new economy. With no old industries to wind down she can leapfrog into the new economy with a well-educated workforce, a beautiful and bountiful environment and, just across the mountains, the example of Bangalore, the e-capital of India, to provide both a model and expertise. It isn't happening. My question to everyone was, 'Why not? If Kerala can't do it, what hope is there for the rest of the developing world?'

The work of the Peruvian economist Hernando de Soto may provide one explanation. His book *The Mystery of Capital* is subtitled 'Why Capitalism Triumphs in the West and Fails Everywhere Else.' The Third World is not short of entrepreneurs, he says. It requires all sorts of ingenuity and enterprise just to survive in those countries. His argument is that the world's poor have all that is necessary for successful capitalism – except capital. He suggests, however, that they do have immense assets; what they lack is the power to turn them into liquid usable capital. The assets of at least 80 per cent of the people of the developing world – their houses, shops and businesses – are not legal and so remain what he calls 'dead capital'.

Because these assets exist in the informal economy and are not registered in any legal property rights system, their owners cannot borrow against them or sell them, they cannot grow their assets and so remain locked into their own *status quo*. The world is now divided between those countries where property rights are widespread and those where the classes are divided between those who can fix property rights and produce capital and those who cannot. Formal property is more than a system for recording assets, it promotes a way of thinking, putting into people's heads the idea of using those assets to create surplus value. We in the West take property rights for granted but, says de Soto, only some twenty-five of the two hundred countries in the world have universal property rights and ways in which work and savings can be converted into usable capital.

To prove his point, de Soto's research team opened a small garment workshop on the outskirts of Lima. They then set about making it legal, standing in queues to see officials, filling in forms, travelling into the city by bus to meet officials. They spent six hours a day at it and eventually registered the business

– 289 days later. They planned to employ only one worker, but the cost of registration was $1,231, thirty-one times the minimum wage. No wonder most micro-businesses don't even bother to try. In the Philippines, if a person has built a dwelling on either state or privately-owned urban land it would need 168 steps, involving fifty-three private and public agencies and taking thirteen to twenty-five years to purchase it legally. In Egypt it will take anywhere from six to eleven years to register a dwelling built on agricultural land. That is why 4.7 million Egyptians have chosen to build their dwellings illegally.

De Soto's statistics continue, the Mexican National Statistics Institute estimated in 1994 that there were 2.65 million informal micro-businesses in the country, none of them legally registered. It is much the same in the old communist regimes. In 1995 *Business Week* estimated that only some 280,000 farmers out of 10 million in Russia owned their own land.

Add up the value of all the illegal assets in a country, often not more than shacks, and you reach astronomical sums. De Soto calculates that the value of extra-legal property in Peru is some $74 billion, five times the total value of the Lima Stock Exchange. In Egypt it would be $240 billion or thirty times the value of the Cairo Stock Exchange and fifty-five times the value of all foreign investments in the country. Adding it up for the Third World as a whole he comes to a figure of $9.3 trillion.

America was once again fortunate in its legacy. The first settlers brought with them an acute awareness of property and were careful to document all their early stakeholdings. But, says, de Soto, only those twenty-five countries with universal property rights produce capital in sufficient quantity to benefit from the expanding global markets. The rest of the world consumes their products but feels excluded from the club of the rich. The answer is to reform the legal process as de Soto set about doing in Peru, to make it easier to own property and therefore to release capital for the natural entrepreneurs of the informal micro-businesses.

De Soto does not directly address India's problems, but C. K. Prahalad does, in an inspiring paper published originally on the

Internet and available therefore to many beyond the academic world in which he works. Prahalad's paper takes as its starting point the possibility that the teeming millions of India's poor could be a profitable market for big business, provided the firms rethought their whole business process.

Prahalad uses, as an example, the decision by Hindustan Lever to follow a local competitor, Nirma, into the low end of the detergent market, a market that HL had assumed could never afford its products. They started by dramatically reducing the oil-to-water ratio in the product, thereby lowering the pollution associated with washing clothes in rivers and other public systems, and greatly reducing the cost. They decentralized production, marketing and distribution to take advantage of the abundant labour pool in rural India. Not only did they make money, they brought a whole chain of small businesses into the formal business arena. Unilever, the parent company, has since repeated the experiment successfully in Brazil with the Ala brand.

To lift them from the bottom of the pyramid the poor need income earning potential and access to credit. Here the examples of community banks like the Grameen Bank started by Mohammad Yunus in Bangladesh or the Shorebank Corporation in Chicago can help. Both have proved that lending money to the poor by those who know them is not necessarily a risky business. Ninety-nine per cent of the Grameen Bank's micro-loans are repaid. De Soto's proposals could provide the basis for more of that credit, while Prahalad's ideas could offer them business opportunities as part of a corporate network of micro-businesses involved in selling low cost products to the poor.

Would these ideas help Kerala? I find it hard to believe that, if given half a chance, the bright, alert people whom I met there could not do more than run their probably unregistered shops and taxi businesses. It's possible, however, that alchemy is schooled out of them by the educational system, still built on lines inherited from the British, and a tradition of conformity rather than experiment. I am tempted to suggest that Kerala got the wrong sort of British, the colonial administrators who wanted to plant British traditions in a foreign soil, not ones like the radical Puritans who went to America to build a society very different from the one they left.

More interesting from my point of view is the possibility that the Keralites are attached to the wrong model of capitalism for their stage of development. The individualist Anglo-American type of capitalism will lead people to seek their own futures wherever they may fare best, which in many cases will be away from Kerala. Even if they were to return, their individualist concerns might do more damage than good in a place that is still socialist at heart.

The guided capitalism of Singapore would seek to lock them into the future of Kerala, persuading them to hitch their fortunes to those of Kerala. It is the sort of capitalism that, I should have thought, would appeal to the socialist government of the state but it needs a leader, an alchemist, with the passion and vision of Lee Kuan Yew to deliver it, and alchemists are rare in Kerala.

I went to Kerala to see how global capitalism was impacting on this beautiful corner of the developing world, with its reputation for well-educated people and far-sighted government. I discovered that it was, to my surprise, a mirror of the world that I had come from, with many of the same dilemmas. Education sets you free, but erodes your commitment to a place, a country or even an organization. Wealth made from beauty can destroy beauty. What is good for the individual may be bad for society. Progress at best is two steps forward, one step back.

Two memories from another part of India came back to me then. Three years earlier we had been travelling in the tea gardens in the foothills of the Himalayas as the guests of a group of tea companies. Tea gardens are beautiful places, acres of camellia bushes whose leaves are picked by hand. They are remote places, so that the tea companies have to house their workers in company villages. Our enlightened hosts also provided modern health care and excellent schools. The boys and girls were immaculate in their school uniforms and were, we were told, doing well in their tests. It was all good to witness, but would this next generation, I wondered, want to work in the tea gardens when they grew up, or would they flee to the big cities? Were not the companies damaging their own future by educating what might have been their next workforce? Probably, they agreed, but what else could enlightened employers do? Would it have been tolerable to keep them illiterate?

Later we learnt of problems with the elephants, real elephants these, not my metaphorical ones. They are running out of jungle as the tea estates expand their acreage. They need to eat some six tons of foliage per day and, desperate to find it, they come at night and rampage through the tea gardens. Attracted by the smell of the liquor that the villagers drink, the elephants can trample down the huts of the villagers, maiming or killing those who can't get out of their way. The villagers try to frighten them away, banging drums and waving lights, but are not allowed to shoot them, elephants being a protected species. The dilemma is clear. The tea estates are the only sizeable employers around. To provide more work, even to stand still, they need to expand. This commercial expansion inevitably damages the natural environment and the habitat of the elephants, who then wreak their havoc on the villages. What to do? No one knows. Commerce and conservation, both good in themselves, are at loggerheads.

These Indian memories are two parables of development. The best of intentions lead to unintended problems. There are no easy answers, in India or elsewhere.

And capitalism? How did I feel after my series of encounters with it around the world? I have little doubt that capitalism breeds innovation. Without the chance to turn ideas into profit many of those ideas would languish in the minds of the individuals who thought of them. Many scientific breakthroughs would still be left in the laboratories of the institutes and universities where they were made, recorded only in the pages of scientific journals. More people now are healthier, live longer and more comfortably (except in parts of Russia and Africa), can do more, go to more places and enjoy more options for their lives, because of capitalism. Eight hundred million Chinese peasants more than doubled their income in ten years after the economy was opened up in 1978. That has to be good. Economic growth makes things possible. Without it there can be no progress of any sort.

Global capitalism also makes a few of us happier. Ironically it is the poor rather than the rich who say that wealth brings happiness. In a series of surveys around the world there is some evidence that a per capita income of $10,000 a year is the point of diminishing returns. Below that level, roughly where Greece and Portugal are today, more money buys more of the basic comforts of life and increases one's satisfaction. Above that level any additional dollars don't appear to make us more cheerful, probably because we are now into rat-race territory, comparing ourselves with our neighbours, or with what we could be, rather than where we came from.

The system also produces a lot of trash and *chindogu*, it encourages selfishness and envy, rewards success sometimes disproportionately and results, often, in greater inequality both within societies and between them. John Micklethwait and Adrian Wooldridge, the authors of *Future Perfect*, a book that mostly celebrates globalization, quote a *Guardian* headline to illustrate the point. 'What is the difference between Tanzania and Goldman Sachs? One is an African country that makes $2.2 billion a year and shares it among 25 million people. The other is an investment bank that makes $2.6 billion and shares it between 161 people.' In 1998, even in a time of great prosperity, American firms found it necessary to sack 677,795 people. I don't like any of these outcomes but we can do something about them, if we so choose. I don't like, either, the frenetic pace that globalization brings, the 24/7 lifestyle of the people that Micklethwait and Wooldridge call the 'cosmocrats'.

I find it hard, however, to feel sorry for this particular 'anxious elite' who face 'the perils of placelessness' because it is a self-inflicted form of luxurious masochism. I do worry, however, that we are all replacing friends with acquaintances and that the erosion of social capitalism that concerns some Americans is spreading across the world. Instead of involving themselves with their neighbours the rich choose to pay taxes to the state, demanding of governments that they clear the streets of crime and improve the schools without giving them enough money to do it, while tucking their own wealth away in international hidey-holes, insulating themselves in their guarded compounds from other people's problems. Capitalism is a powerful river. If it is allowed to overflow its banks it floods everything around it. Strong flood defences are needed, from governments and from international organizations, and from ourselves.

It is true, too, that the speed of change in modern capitalism has heightened insecurity, for businesses as well as for individuals. It means that what worked last year may not be good enough this year, that last year's project is now a yellowing file, that those in authority quickly become yesterday's people, that it is impossible to plan too far ahead or to know who or what to rely on. Not everything changes for the better. That may be exciting for the young and competent, but for most people it is just uncomfortable and worrying. Economic growth means that we travel further and faster and linger less, have less time to stand and stare or to care for our neighbours. Slow down the world, I want to get off, we say to ourselves. Well, we can if we so choose.

We could also decide to go another way. The new rich might cultivate stealth wealth, paying for upmarket organic food and spare living, for more discrimination rather than more consumption. It might become chic not to travel but to walk the pathways nearer home, to demand better public transport rather than smarter cars. Divorce could come to be seen as socially selfish, requiring more houses in a Britain already too heavily built upon. Junk food and conspicuous consumption could become as socially unacceptable as smoking is in parts of America.

Capitalism is, however, the only game in town. Even if we wanted to, there is no way to stop it. We can tame it only to some extent. If, in 2021, we want to look back on twenty years of progress then we need a new ideology, a new politics of generosity and openness, a creed that insists on our common human tradition and a willingness to build a society that works for us all, not just for a few. That requires imaginative leadership, and tough discipline. Without that sort of leadership there is a real fear that what the American specialist in international affairs Edward Luttwalk calls turbo capitalism will lead to a form of fascism as the impoverished unite in the sort of populism that brought Hitler to power.

For capitalism to work and not shoot itself in the foot, we have to make it work for more people, everywhere. It should concern us that the benefits of capitalism are concentrated on the elites of the world's middle classes, perhaps two billion at the most out of what will be ten billion people in total by the end of this century. It is no good just giving the other eight billion money to spend, remittance money. We must give them the chance to earn money, real money. Otherwise many of those eight billion are going to behave like the Keralites, they will go where the honey is, to the First World where the population is ageing and declining. Migration is set to be the major issue of this century, unless we can make it more attractive for everyone to remain in their own Keralas. In our own interests we must make capitalism succeed in the developing world. We must find ways to give the poor more of the choices that we have, even the right to make the wrong choices.

Back home, we must get better at making those choices ourselves. The best way to predict the future, said the management guru Peter Drucker, is to invent it. Don't compete: do something different, redefine what winning means. Capitalism at least gives us that possibility. I admit that when we are being washed away in a flood it is hard to think of choice, but a flood may sometimes sweep us to a new place and new possibilities.

Like the Puritans arriving in the wilds of America there is then the chance to create a New Found Land. At the end of my journeys I reflected that if we could combine the energy and self-confidence of the Americans, the charm and friendliness of the Keralites and the disciplined determination of the Singporeans to build a better future for their society, we would be making the best of capitalism.

That, however, would be a cross-cultural miracle. More pragmatically, I began to realize, the real challenge for capitalism is to achieve the right balance between ends and means. In miniature, it was the sort of challenge that I faced when I first arrived in Windsor Castle to run the conference and study centre that was St George's House. I inherited an institution where the prevailing philosophy was the need to live within our means, but it seemed to me and my colleagues that life would be easier if we could increase the means, giving us more room to manoeuvre. We therefore invited some corporations to use it as a retreat centre for their boards and top managers, paying us the sort of fees they might have had to pay for one of their more accustomed conference hotels. This was, however, a more blatantly commercial use of the centre than its founders had envisaged and not everyone was pleased.

It did, nevertheless, relieve the financial pressures and allow us to subsidize other parts of our work. The problem, I then saw, was getting the balance right. It was financially seductive to increase the new corporate lettings, but that would short-change our original mission, which was to bring together individuals of influence across the divides of society to debate together the ethical and moral issues of our time. Groups of cigar-chomping executives talking among themselves did not fit that definition. Too much attention to the means of the place, the need to pay the bills, would deflect us from our ends. On the other hand, neglecting the money to run the place would undermine our purpose. Getting the right balance meant denying ourselves some more easy income in order to do what we were meant to do.

Writ large, society has the same sort of challenge. Maximizing wealth creation as a priority can mean that we forget the reasons why we wanted it. Too much concentration on the ideology, on the other hand, can lead to a neglect of the means. Communism had a great purpose – the equality of all in the pursuit of a better society for all – but had no way to deliver it, no effective means. Capitalism knows all about the means of wealth creation but is unclear about the ends, who or what that wealth should be for. That may yet be its downfall.

In the third part of this book I will try to describe how I set about dealing with the dilemmas of choice that capitalism offers, as well as the need to balance means and ends in my own life. Eventually I began to invent my own future. I will also suggest what we will have to do as a society in order to help more people to do likewise.

PART III

THE INDEPENDENT LIFE

7

THE PROBLEMS OF THE
PORTFOLIO LIFE

In the first year of my independence our Christmas office party was a dinner for two.

I was free, but I was also alone. Aloneness is not necessarily loneliness, but neither is it belonging. Fleas don't flock. They may feed off bigger creatures but they don't and can't live inside them. I rejoiced, that first year of independence, in the fact that my name now appeared on those lists of attendees at conferences or meetings with a blank space opposite it instead of an organization. I was my own man, not the representative of something else. Come the end-of-year celebrations, however, and the dearth of invitations to this or that departmental bash was only too obvious.

A wonderful relief, I told myself. No more false jollity over the paper cups of cheap wine, no need to feign bonhomie with colleagues whom I had been avoiding all year. But the truth was that I missed the invitations. This was death by social exclusion. Better to be invited and hate the going than be invited at all. If I don't belong anywhere, I began to ask myself, do I matter any more to anyone? Is there any point to my existence? Office parties may not merit such existential worries but they have been one of the modern world's symbols of community. That sort of community had died for me now.

The death of the old is no bad thing as long as it is followed by new life. I had felt imprisoned by my organizations and needed to escape, but like most of us I was not made to be a hermit. We were made, it seems, to hunt in packs and to live in tribes, and having left the nest of the organization I needed to find somewhere else to belong, some others to hunt with. I would have to invent my own ways of belonging – to something.

What was true for me is true for every flea, young or old. The tension between wanting to belong and needing to be free never goes away. Fleas (the insect, order *Siphonaptera*) are generally regarded as parasites. Organisms do not exactly invite them in, would prefer to get rid of them if they could. The independent life may be the way of the future for many, but they can't count on being part of any community, unless they make the positive decision to join one for part of their time, or, better still, to create one as our alchemists had done.

I had not expected this. I had felt so imprisoned in most of the communities of my life – schools, organizations, families, villages – that it had never occurred to me that I might miss them. I am an extreme case. As a writer I jealousy guard the allocation of my time, and the freedom to speak my own mind. I join nothing these days, not even a political party or a golf club. My relationships with organizations now are mostly spasmodic, tangential and temporary, being built around isolated events or projects. I am an outworker, and outworkers don't belong. If I wanted an organization to belong to I would have to create my own.

That wasn't going to happen. I had no need of an organization to do my work. Instead, with Elizabeth, I have had to create a private network or quasi-community. Some of that community comes from our work, some from the private side of our life. These, together with our close family, are the people who truly matter to us, to whom we are committed and to whom, I hope, we matter a little. Those personal networks, however, are not self-maintaining. They need to be worked at. Fortunately, I am blessed by having a social broker as my wife and partner. A flea by instinct, she has never worked in an organization and has always understood that she would have to create her own communities of both work and private life. She works hard at keeping in touch with a wide range of friends. E-mail helps, but best of all are their knees under our table, eating, drinking, talking.

Left to myself, I would wait for the telephone to ring, because you do need some social energy, even some self-confidence, to pick up that phone yourself and issue an invitation. Who knows, the person at the other end might reject your overtures or, worse, might not remember who you are. Left to myself I would probably join clubs and associations instead, would go to conferences and meetings, might seek election as a club officer, even as a churchwarden of the parish church. I fear, however, that it is not always their interests that I would have at heart. I would be looking for a tribe to belong to. Many of those who volunteer their services to some charity or other are likewise doing it as much to meet their own needs for belonging as to serve the cause. Belonging matters.

Just as I had not expected to miss community, nor had I anticipated the next tension, this one more philosophical than social. Now that I was free to shape my own future, to set my own goals, I had to give some serious thought to what my life was all about. It was a question that I had encountered at intervals in the past, as when I stood by my father's grave, but now I realized that if I had to plan my own life I needed more than a gut reaction, I needed a strategy. But I also knew that for any strategy to be rooted enough to work it had to spring from a sense of mission, an underlying purpose. Without that driving purpose I would be like many of the businesses I had encountered, planning only to survive, to get through the next year. Survival, I felt, was not going to be sufficient justification for a life; well, not for my life, even if it does well enough for some businesses. As far as I am concerned this life is the only thing we have to play with so we had better do something useful with it. Was it in my genes, I have sometimes wondered, or due to those early days in the vicarage, this burdensome compulsion to take life so seriously? All I know is that I could never be content to idle my way to death.

Most mornings in our London flat we entertain someone to breakfast. A strange American aberration, my British friends call it, amazed at our uncivilized behaviour. The guests, we explain, are typically young people in a hurry, wanting to discuss their careers or, more often now, the new ventures they are proposing or helping to start. Breakfast doesn't interfere with their day, and if they can manage to get to Putney by 8.30 a.m. they must, we feel, want to come! I ask them one question to start with: why? Why are they contemplating this or that course or venture? I learn a lot from their answers. Many respond that it just seems a good idea. I know then that they won't do it, or that if they do, it won't succeed.

We tell them then about the alchemists whom we met in our study. Passion was what drove them, a passionate belief in what they were doing, a passion that sustained them through the tough times, that seemed to justify their life. Passion is a much stronger word than mission or purpose, and I realize as I speak that I am also talking to myself. Passionate people move mountains where missionaries can only preach.

'How do you find this passion?' they ask.

'In dreams,' I often reply. 'We all dream in our sleep, but some dream in the daytime. Such people are dangerous, because they can make their dreams come true.' Most of us have a dream of what we might be, or do or create. If it's a vague dream, such as to be really rich, or to have a large family or just to be happy, then it is more hope than dream. Passion is not born of vague hopes.

Rummaging in a drawer not long ago I came across the New Year resolutions that we had individually made as a family twenty-two years ago. Our then young teenage daughter had resolved to make no more resolutions! But Elizabeth had written, 'To spend more time on my passion, photography.' At this time she was working as a marriage counsellor, there had been no thought of the long degree course in photography that she embarked on three years later, and no idea that she would become a distinguished portrait photographer with three photographic books already published. Ask her now, as some do, why she took up photography in midlife and she will say, 'It was something that I always dreamt of doing, even when I was a young girl with a box camera.'

I'm ashamed to say that twenty-two years ago I had dismissed her passion as a hobby and had done nothing to encourage her, but the dream and the passion were always there, just waiting.

It is easier to see the passion in others than to find it in oneself. I don't think of myself as a passionate person – more dispassionate and cool, I would say, shy and tentative, unless I am up on a platform in role. I did have a dream, however, one that turned into a quiet passion. My dream was to write, although I concealed it from myself for many years, trying to be something that I wasn't, a business executive. I had also discovered along the way that I was, at heart, a teacher. So it was inevitable, I suppose, that my first book was a textbook. It would be nice, I often think, to be able to write a novel, even a play, but I know I won't because the passion for that isn't there. And a nice idea is not enough.

Some are lucky and discover their dream early on. I often envy those who know at fifteen that they want to be a doctor, or are instinctive entrepreneurs who loved creating enterprises even while at school. Ellen MacArthur, the young British woman who sailed alone around the world in record time in 2001, was making a dream come true, a dream that started when she was a small child. 'I hope,' she said when she made port after ninety-four days alone on the oceans, 'that this will encourage other young people to live their dreams.'

On the other hand, submerged dreams, like mine, do allow one to experience other aspects of life. I have no regrets about my abortive business career. I learnt a lot along the way. Our daughter Kate started life as a would-be architect, fell ill, so abandoned architecture and started a small business, fell out with her partner and went to teach English to Italians in Rome. It was only then that her submerged dream of being a healer came through. She did a four-year course in osteopathy which she now practises with great success and fulfilment. She has no regrets. She even said once that she was grateful for her illness. It forced her to stop in her tracks, to adjust her priorities and, these days, helps her to empathize with her patients.

Some stumble on their passions. After my dreadful schooling the last thing I wanted to be was a teacher. Then by chance Shell made me one, but of willing adults, not reluctant schoolboys. I loved it, and what you love you are often good at. So, to those who have not found a passion, I now find myself saying, 'experiment, try anything that takes your fancy, but until it turns into a passion don't make it the centre of your life, because it won't last'.

If the lack of a community and the need for a passion were the first two unexpected tensions in my new life as a flea, the third should have been easy to anticipate, given my background. That was the need to keep learning, growing, developing. Whatever you do as an independent you are only as good as your last job or project or creation.

I once told a fellow author that I was working on a new book and was finding it hard to plough new furrows in a new field.

'Really?' he said. 'Most of us just write the same book again and call it something else.'

That won't be true of me, I determined, but of course it has turned out just as he said. Re-reading my first book written twenty-five years ago, I was dismayed at first to find how many of what I had thought were original ideas in later books had first surfaced there in some form. I later came to think that I should not be too ashamed. If you are writing about the same topics it is unlikely that you are going to change your views too frequently or too radically. What you hope is that the old ideas are still relevant but need to be reinterpreted to fit the new realities, that there will be new insights to offer, new perspectives, new experiences to share.

The same is true of every type of work. We don't expect the

surgeon to change all his techniques, or to switch his focus from stomachs to brains. What we do expect is that he keeps abreast of the research, even contributes to it, updates his procedures and remains open to new ideas. It would need to be the same for me.

In my days in the elephants learning had been hard to avoid. It was organized, required and available in one form or another. I was sent on courses, although I learnt most from being forced to face up to my mistakes on the job. In academia I was supposed to spend a fifth of my time keeping up with my area of expertise and adding to it in some way; indeed, advancement depended more on my colleagues' assessment of my research than on my teaching. In the study centre at Windsor my days mostly consisted of listening to experts from other worlds, much of it interesting, some fascinating, all relevant to my then purpose of understanding the dilemmas of the society we lived in.

Now, independent, unattached, in command of my own time, I had to do it myself. Furthermore, it wasn't going to be paid for! I started by reading everything written by my competitors. Business books, I came to the conclusion, were often full of good notions but were deadly dull to read. I remembered my own advice to entrepreneurs, not to try to do better, but to do different. I also remembered writing that first textbook – on understanding organizations – in a farmhouse in Southern France. I had filled the boot of the car with all the best business books then around, most of them American academic textbooks. I found them sterile. They didn't answer many of the questions that I wanted to pose. They reduced humanity to numbers, passion and desire to a hierarchy of needs. Depressed by their arid prose I gave up my book and decided to spend my time sampling the library of the owner of the farmhouse. She was a fan of the great Russian novelists. I discovered that Tolstoy and Dostoevsky had more to say about the trials and tribulations of individuals in organizations than any of the textbooks. I owe much of my book's subsequent popularity to Tolstoy. It may not have been better than the other books but it was certainly different.

Reflecting on all this I decided that to be different rather than better I would need to step outside my area of expertise if I was going to glean new insights and new ideas. As I had often pointed out to businesses, the real innovations usually come from outside the industry or the firm; those that come from inside are typically developments of the familiar, not truly new. I suspect that this is true for all who want to be different rather than just better. We have to force ourselves to walk in alien worlds from time to time in order to see things afresh or see fresh things.

Then I came across a small book by Donald Schon, an American academic. It was called *The Displacement of Concepts*, not the most sexy of titles but an important idea. It was about creativity in science. His argument was that most of the big breakthroughs in science, relativity for instance, had come from borrowing a concept from one area of life and applying it as a metaphor to another. Do this and you can often see familiar objects in a new way or find a way of linking data that opens new doors, as Crick and Watson famously did with the metaphor of a double helix.

I stopped reading my competitors' books. Instead I burrowed into works of history, into biographies and novels, looking for concepts. Those books are, after all, full of the stuff of life, and life was what I wanted to illuminate. I went to the theatre a lot, remembering those early days at the London Business School. Shakespeare, I realized shamefacedly, had already said a lot of it much better. Encouraged by Elizabeth I began to understand a little more about art, opera and music. These were all areas of our cultural heritage that I had not found time for in the past, alien worlds waiting for me to walk in them. Life hitherto had been too occupied in trying to do better, even just to keep up. We made a rule when visiting a city of one restaurant for every gallery or museum visited. She chose the gallery, I chose the restaurant. Learning can be fun, although fattening!

Foreign countries, too, can be schools of a sort. We are bad tourists, believing that you see more of the reality of a culture by living or working in it, rather than just looking at it. The work that I do seldom lasts more than a week in one place, but even in that short time we do get to see behind the façade of a culture. You are treated differently if you are working rather than sightseeing. In the old days, Shell would encourage anyone going abroad for a meeting to make sure that they also took time out while they were there to go to an opera or concert, to walk the streets and meet the local people, preferably people other than their opposite numbers. In the new time-precious world the executives fly in and out, often not venturing beyond the airport hotel.

America, Singapore and India gave me new perspectives on life. So did Italy. We spend a lot of time in Italy, one way and another. They do many things differently there, not all of them brilliantly, but there is much to ponder on in those differences. Italians don't travel much. Their country, they feel, has everything that any mortal could need. They are fierce defenders of their culture – their food, their football, their art and their fashion. Once when we were there the whole of Tuscany staged a one-day strike because someone, then unknown, had detonated a bomb in the Uffizi Gallery in Florence. They wanted to demonstrate their outrage at this sort of vandalism. I found it hard to imagine a similar demonstration in London had a bomb gone off in the Tate Gallery. Yet these cultural nationalists are also enthusiastic supporters of the European Union. You can, they feel, be Italian and also European, taking the best from both, albeit ignoring, I also noted, those directives from Brussels that they find objectionable.

Perhaps because Italy as a nation is relatively young, Italians think local and family more than they think national. I vividly recall an Italian journalist being interviewed on BBC Radio during one of the periodic political crises in Rome.

'Is it serious?' the interviewer asked him.

'Yes, it is very serious,' the Italian replied, 'but it is not important. You see,' he went on, 'we live in a golden country under the sun. Life goes on whether the government in Rome is working or not.'

A little too unconcerned, maybe, about the fate of his

government, but we have something to learn from the Italian sense of civic pride in their villages, towns and cities.

The messages from the differences go on.

The Italian economy draws much of its strength from its multitude of small family businesses. How is it, I ask myself, that the Italians talk of family businesses whereas the British call them 'small and medium enterprises'? Is it because the Italians intend the business to last for generations while the British aim to sell them to another and bigger business in due course? The British believe that you have to grow to survive, but many of these Italian firms believe that you can get better without getting bigger.

I am not suggesting that the Italians always have things the right way round, only that the world viewed through an Italian lens can look different, can make you question what you previously took for granted.

It is one thing to find the concepts. I then had to apply them to the illumination of life in and around organizations. I also knew, looking back at my early education by rote, that unused knowledge evaporates, often in weeks if not days. Years of French verbs supposedly committed to memory in the classroom had all gone from my head by the time I got to Paris. Tempting though it was just to pile up all the fun stuff I was encountering, I knew I had to use it in some way or it would disappear. Indeed, I was already finding that I was reading a novel for the second time and not realizing until I was halfway through that I had been there before.

So it was that writing, lecturing and broadcasting became the mortar for my learning, the stuff that made it stick. I would test out the new concepts or metaphors in the lectures. If they seemed to click they would eventually appear in a book. If you can get your customers to pay for your learning everyone benefits. My product is a book, but I believe that the same principles will apply to anyone who wants to do something different rather than just better. Walk in other worlds, look, listen, inquire, then go back and turn it into a new way of

looking at your world, fix the new concept into your conscious-
ness by using it. If it fails to make a difference, discard it
quickly, go look somewhere else.

I was once asked to help the new owner of a medium-sized
food company turn it into a model for the industry by educating
his managers. I think that he had in mind a course of some sort. I
had had my fill of that sort of education. It would be largely a
waste of time, I told him. Instead he should select a small cadre
of the most respected managers and supervisors, people who
could command respect from their colleagues. I would then send
them forth to walk in other worlds, or other organizations in
their case. At least, I assured him, it would help them make their
organization different from the rest of the industry, and that
would make them proud. I fed them with journal articles about
the best of Britain's businesses, asked them to choose a couple
each to go and visit, my job being to help them gain entry. The
only proviso was that none of the businesses should be in their
industry. They went forth, gleaned a pile of new ideas, compared
notes, picked out the ones they found most exciting and put
together a programme of change for their company over the next
two years. It was my most successful corporate educational
programme and I had personally taught them nothing.

I used the same formula in other educational programmes later
on. I called it learning by voyeuring. We are all, maybe, voyeurs
at heart. I suspect like others, I have spent a happy summer
poking my nose into other people's homes under the pretence
that I was a potential buyer. People do live in extraordinary
ways, but some of them gave us ideas for our own home. I have,
half seriously, described myself as an organizational voyeur. It is
a powerful way to learn, provided that it doesn't stop there and
you do something with the ideas you glean.

Belonging, dreaming and learning, these were all new
dilemmas for my new independent life, new only because they
didn't come packaged and assumed in the organizational job.
There were also the very practical dilemmas of independence –
how to organize my work and earn enough money while still
balancing my life between work and home, between Elizabeth's

needs and mine. I discuss these important dilemmas in the next two chapters. But first, and in many ways most crucially of all, at this turning point in my life I had to come to terms with doubt.

The freedom of independence is enticing, but putting your own name to something requires a certain arrogance, whether it's a new little business or a book. For many years I have occasionally been asked to offer a Thought for the Day on the BBC's *Today* programme on the radio. The idea is to provide a religious or moral reflection on one of the issues of the day. Some four million or more listeners regularly tune in to this early morning digest of news and current affairs, even if they are only half attending as they go about their early morning chores. I was flattered to be asked. Politicians would give their eye teeth to be allowed three minutes free of interruptions or questions to air their views to such an audience. Secretly, however, I had to agree with the mother of a good friend who said to her, 'What right does your chum Charles have to impose his views on us unasked over our breakfast table?'

It is the same with putting your name to an article or stepping on to a platform to speak to a few hundred people. By what right, you wonder, do you do this? Everyone I have spoken to who puts their name to their words agrees that one walks a tightrope every time, between exhibiting the self-confidence that convinces and the self-doubt that worries why anyone should want to listen to or read what you have to say. I console myself with the thought that it is a free market – anyone can turn off the radio, throw the book away or leave the conference hall. Nevertheless, just to get started you do have to dredge up a lot of self-belief, the polite term for a private arrogance.

The tightrope never leaves you, in my experience. I would be worried if it did. Self-confident doubt, decent doubt, keeps one honest. I come from a long line of preachers. Perhaps, being ordained, they felt that they were licensed by God to air their views. I don't feel that. For me, it's more a case of 'you've got to do what you've got to do' or, more formally, you have to speak and live the truth as you see it. Doubt or no doubt, it's unsatisfactory to live a lie.

When we first went to Italy I was gobsmacked by the art and architecture of the early Renaissance. It wasn't just that the paintings and sculptures were beautiful, they also contained a clear message. God and his saints had hitherto been the subject matter of all art, lifting our thoughts to things above. In this new art, however, God had been replaced by mankind, by real men and women. Donatello's sculptures may portray saints and prophets but they are very obviously real people – just look at his wood sculpture of Mary Magdalene in the Cathedral Museum in Florence; or the Pieta in that same place, carved by Michelangelo towards the end of his life, in which Christ is very clearly a dead man, not a God.

I was looking at the visual expression of the new humanism, not a rejection of God but a vivid demonstration that He works through us. The idea that God is a spirit within you is common to many religions, and here, for the first time, I was seeing that idea expressed in art. Somehow it was more immediate and more powerful than when it was only a rational argument. I couldn't escape the implications with these powerful images all around me. I am more comfortable thinking of the hidden possibility within me, rather than the parental God of my childhood, but the message is the same: you can't duck the obligations to yourself to live up to the untested possibilities within you. Getting by, surviving, is not enough. Marsilio Ficino, the philosopher of the Renaissance, put it nicely: we are essentially, he says, that which is greatest within us, which he calls the soul. All his writings are an invitation to live up to that greater self.

I remember, although she claims she doesn't, a conversation with my wife soon after we married, when I was working in London for Shell, educating their managers.

'Are you proud of your work?' she asked one evening.

'It's all right, as work goes.'

'What about the people you work with, are they special?'

'They're all right.'

'So, the company, Shell, is it really a good organization doing good things?'

'I can't complain, it's all right.'

She looked hard at me, then said, 'I don't think I want to spend the rest of my life with someone who is prepared to settle for all right.'

It was an ultimatum of sorts and I resigned from Shell the next month, but the conversation has always rung in my ears. 'All right' is not enough. I agree. We have only one life, we need to do more with it than merely survive. But what? And what is life about, in the end? The question still niggles.

8

CHUNKING THE WORK

There was, in the first weeks of my fleadom, that strange delight of looking at a blank appointments diary, of realizing that I could cross out days and weeks for holidays or private activities without consulting my colleagues. I remember going to do the shopping one weekday afternoon and feeling like a guilty schoolboy, because it was something that I had never done before on a working day. Odd too, to find so many other men of working age doing the same. And how come, I suddenly thought, that there are always crowds at the races in midweek? They can't all be retired, and the unemployed would be too poor.

Maybe there have always been people who lived my new sort of life. It was just that I was never around to see them. When I was speaking about the portfolio lifestyle to a group of executives later that year, one of them seemed dubious.

'Where are they, these so-called portfolio people?' he said, 'I don't see any of them on the 8.10 from Weybridge in the morning.'

'No,' I replied, 'portfolio people rarely need to travel on

crowded rush hour trains. You won't see them around, not because they aren't there but because you aren't.'

It's an old story. We see what we want to see in the world around us. We read the newspapers that support our views and prejudices, we work and socialize with people like ourselves. We don't, most of us, go to the other side of town, or talk to strangers in the train. We only know how others live by watching sagas on TV. Until I had shaken off the bonds of the office my view of the world was largely an unchecked stereotype. It was exciting, and humbling, to find that there was another whole world out there that didn't check into offices or factories every morning, that set its own timetables and priorities, that mixed paid work and other work in all sorts of combinations, whose days weren't governed by meetings and committees, to whom multi-tasking wasn't a new management buzzword but a fact of ordinary life.

'You're getting real at last,' said Elizabeth. 'Most women have always lived a multi-tasking life. You may call it portfolio living, I call it getting on with things.'

Very soon, however, my empty appointments diary was not a delight but a worry. Euphoria turned to panic. Organizations, I began to see, may be prisons of a sort but they do have one huge advantage in that they channel work your way, sending a stream of duties, tasks, opportunities and challenges down the phone, through the fax or e-mail, out of meeting rooms and even from chance encounters in the corridors, into one's in-tray. Most of my time in organizations had been consumed by that notional in-tray, the things that had to be attended to; my constant, but mostly unrealized, ambition had been to move beyond it, to do things undreamt or unthought of by others.

Now was my chance, because that in-tray was empty. No mail, no telephone calls, no meetings, no deadlines, nothing. But a life without deadlines, I was discovering, is a life without any priorities. There is no pressure to do anything, and the deadlines that you set yourself are too easily revised or abandoned. I began to feel very unwanted, almost as if I didn't exist. Role underload, I had pointed out in an early book, was often more stressful than role overload. Now I was discovering for myself how true that could be. Dickens went for fifteen-mile walks when he was depressed. I was too lazy. 'So this is what it feels like to be unemployed,' I thought, making a note of it for possible future use. I could have signed on at the Job Centre, but I was not available for work, as they would have required, at least not the sort of work they might have to offer.

It was time to apply my own theories about work to myself, to practise some of the ideas that I had been preaching from the safety of secure jobs. Work, I believed, was a fundamental part of life. No one should live without it. As I was discovering in my new existence, life without work was a life without a point. The mistake, my mistake, was to think that there was only one form of work, namely paid work – the job. That ignores and demeans all the other sorts of work and the people who do it. Such a narrow definition of work puts the economic needs of society ahead of all the other purposes of our existence. I like money as much as anyone, it is important stuff, particularly if it's lacking, but it should not be the whole point of life. The language of work was distorting society, I believed. I had wanted to correct that by emphasizing the other three types of work, familiar to all of us but either taken for granted or dismissed as unimportant by most. A sensible life would contain chunks of all three types, in a balanced work portfolio.

There is, for instance, home work, by which I'm not referring to school days, but all the work that goes on in the home – the cooking and cleaning, the caring and rearing, the repairing and fixing, the gardening and the driving. Employ outsiders to do all these tasks, as some do, and the costs are huge. A live-in nanny in London may expect, today, her own apartment and car on top of a salary of £20,000. A neighbour in the country pays his gardener £22,000 a year and claims he is worth every penny. There are firms that will clean your home on a regular basis, cooks who prepare all your meals and others who will walk the dog, change your light bulbs and drive your car. The parents are ageing? There are homes aplenty to take them and your money off your hands. It would not be difficult to spend £100,000 a year contracting out all the home work, much to the benefit of the economy and the employment statistics.

Most of us, however, do it ourselves, for free. And most of the 'us' are still women. No wonder they want some financial recognition, if not in the form of a salary, then in the form of tax concessions. It won't happen, because it would cost too much, but no one would want to deny that home work is an immensely valuable and important aspect of work. It needs to be officially counted as work in the statistics because, unfortunately, what is not counted does not count. Its rewards come in the form of (mostly unspoken) gratitude and love, of the sense of a home created and maintained, a place of belonging, an island in a turbulent world. Intangible rewards, no doubt, but ones to be treasured when they happen. Those of us who do little of it are missing something. A balanced life should surely include a good chunk of home work, for both sexes. Portfolio working, the independent life of a flea, gives us that chance if we choose to so arrange things.

Then there is gift work, the work that we also do for free, but this time outside the home, in the community or the world at large. Surveys suggest that most of us do some of this work at some stage in our lives. Some do it through organizations, others more informally. Not everyone in Britain realizes that the lifeboats around our coasts are manned for free by volunteers, as are the mountain rescue teams who also risk their lives to save others. Less dramatically the people who staff the Citizens Advice Bureaux, deliver Meals on Wheels or service the Crisis centres for the homeless at Christmas are giving chunks of their lives to help the less fortunate. The list is endless – churches and charity shops, youth clubs and campaigning groups, all dependent on gift work to do their job, some 250,000 voluntary organizations or charities in Britain alone.

Most of the time the work I do for free is the most satisfying. I do it because I believe in it, not because I need to for financial reasons, or because I am required by someone else to do it. But first I had to dump the bits of gift work where I was contributing nothing useful, using the organizations more for what they could give me than for what I could give them. I had been seduced by the lure of status and had given my time to some worthy organizations, but mostly, I fear, sitting on their councils or committees rather than working on the ground. When I came to terms with the fact that organizations were not my métier and that I ended up either bored or bolshie in meetings, I decided to resign.

I wrote seven resignation letters in one day but received only three in return, acknowledging my resignation and thanking me for my services. The others had either not noticed my participation or were just pleased to be rid of me! It would be more sensible, I decided, to offer for free the few things that I did best rather than the things I did badly. Too many people use voluntary organizations as a chance to do what no one in their senses would ever pay them to do, such as chairing committees or managing the finances. I resolved that I would confine myself to offering to write or speak or listen – that way I wouldn't do too much harm.

Lastly, there is study work. It is fashionable these days to talk of lifelong learning, but few of us take any steps to make it happen. Yet in a changing world we cannot rely on what we used to know to see us through the future. When I entered academia I was told that I was expected to spend the equivalent of one day a week on research, and that I would be judged on my output of new knowledge or new thinking in my field. It seemed only sensible that those who teach should be expected to keep up with the field and, if possible, ahead of it. Come to think of it, why should that not apply to all those whose job it is to keep ahead of the competition in business, or up with best practice in all the professions?

Twenty per cent of one's time spent on keeping abreast of the field might be too much for many, so I used to suggest that a minimum of 10 per cent, or twenty-five days a year, of study in some form or other, should be required of any competent executive or professional, some of which could reasonably be expected to be done in the individual's own time. Ten years ago the average business executive spent one day a year in any formal kind of study. Few had the time or energy to read books or professional journals or to attend conferences. Organizations preferred to compartmentalize their forward thinking in research departments or planning groups, but the new thinking seldom infected the hearts and minds of the principle decision-makers, who then often found themselves left behind in the race to the future.

Independent fleas have only themselves to rely on. Study work was going to be essential, I realized, if there was to be any future for my paid work. In my case the focus of the study would be my writing. Most writers, novelists included, spend about three times as many hours or weeks researching their work as they do actually writing.

When I started my new life I retreated to the country to write. We look out on a cornfield and delight in watching it change from brown to green to gold as the months go by. But every fifth year, to our distress, the farmer grows beet or beans: not nearly so pleasant to look out on. There was even the year when he grew nothing. We suggested that surely crop rotation was outmoded in these days of fertilizers. 'The ground needs the occasional change as well as invigoration,' he said, 'and some fallow time to give it a real rest.'

Me too, I reflected. One of the joys of portfolio work is that it is a form of crop rotation. Study work also, I find, is greatly enriched by some fallow time. Write too much too quickly and I only have to delete it all the next day. Read too voraciously one evening and I have to read it all over again later on. Some days I read and write, some days I sit and think, and some days I just sit. It can be hard to explain to a busy world.

Every day the local farmer would go past in his tractor on the way to his fields. He would wave. I would look up from my chair and wave back. One day he stopped.

'That's a nice life you have,' he said, 'just sitting there all day.'

'It's my work,' I said, 'it's how I earn my money.'

'Funny sort of work if you ask me,' he snorted as he started up his tractor again. Yet I knew that he would spend that evening catching up on crop prices or the latest EU subsidies, or leafing through his farming magazines for news of new machinery or seed varieties. Only, he wouldn't call that work. Work for him was physical toil, whereas physical exertion for me was 'exercise', what I do to refresh my mind and body for my real work, with my books.

The mix of the four types of work will vary over the course of a life cycle. In my thirties paid work predominated in my portfolio, much to the despair of my wife who was left with almost all the home work. Fifteen years earlier it had been study work. At the other end of life it is commonplace to hear a retired person say that he has never been busier, but on investigation he has usually swapped the bulk of his paid work for the other three types of work, and found them at least equally fulfilling. We do not, however, have to let our stage in life determine our mix of work. We can create our own mix of work, our own balance of the four types. I was now free, not retired, not employed, not ill or unfit. If anyone was in a position to put my theories to the test it was me.

I sat down with Elizabeth to work out an appropriate mix. It was not something I could do on my own because she would inevitably be affected by the result. After all, she had her own work portfolio to think of.

We decided that I needed to allocate a hundred days a year to my study work, that is to my writing and the preparation for it – all that reading. This would be the foundation of all the paid work that I would do. It was crucial that I gave it enough time. It was too risky to try to live on any intellectual capital from my past. I had heard it said of one of my colleagues that some people knew his lecture off by heart, they had heard it so often.

Nor could I rely on earning any real money from the books that might result from that study work. Most books, I knew, sold fewer than five thousand copies spread over a couple of years, and it was going to take at least two years before any book could be published, even if I could find a publisher. 'Don't fool yourself,' said my first, and only, literary agent, when I told him that I was giving up my day job, 'you'll be very lucky indeed if you ever earn as much as £10,000 in any year from writing.'

Twenty years on I can count myself fortunate. I found a publisher, two of them in fact, and they have served me very well. One or two of the books have even sold many more copies than the five thousand that I might have expected, but I still cannot rely on any future book doing likewise. I still categorize my writing days as study work and any money that results as a bonus.

I knew I would have to earn my real money some other way. Like many former executives I thought of consultancy. Perhaps people would be glad to have my advice even if they couldn't have my management skills. I had forgotten that it was a long time since I had been an executive in a business and a few years since I professed to teach management. The clients did not exactly queue up, and the only contract on offer turned out to be a disaster. A much admired friend and chief executive of a major charity asked me to help him reorganize his management team. It wasn't working, he said.

'To be truthful,' he confided, 'I would like to get rid of them all, but in a charity, that's not so easy. See what you can do.' I spent some weeks immersing myself in the organization, talking to as many people in and around it as I could, including the board. My conclusion was sad but, I felt, unavoidable. The problem lay with my friend himself, a brilliant intellect and public speaker, but an insensitive manager and leader. 'He runs the place by remote control,' they all told me. 'We don't know what goes on in his mind. We no longer trust him or have confidence in his decisions.'

I told him this as gently as I could and suggested some ways in which he could retrieve his reputation. It was no good. He angrily rejected my analysis. There was a bitter argument between us in front of the board. I remember telling them that trust was like a sheet of glass – once broken it could never be the same again no matter how hard you tried to glue it together. It was a cruel thing to say and it proved to be fatal. He resigned that night. He never forgave me, or spoke to me again. I had lost a friend and I could not swear that I had helped the organization. I made two resolves: that I would never again work for a friend as client, and that I would never again try to play God in an organization. Consultancy was not, I sensed, going to be my forte.

It was one more instance of coming to terms with what I was not in order to concentrate on what I was. If money was needed then what I was good at was teaching, particularly managers. Teaching might mean going back to the world I had left but it would be the most efficient way to earn the core money I needed to support my family. I would then be free to do what I really wanted to do – to write. Portfolio people often have to mix the necessary and the desirable. I remember the woman I met who, when I asked what she did, replied that she wrote TV plays. I expressed my admiration.

'Oh, none of them have yet been performed,' she said.

'What do you live on then?' I asked, ever curious about other people's lives.

'I pack eggs on Sundays,' she replied with a smile.

The way she earned her money was not, in her mind, her real work.

It was, for me, an important little conversation. I had grown up assuming that work had to deliver everything in one package – money, satisfaction, companionship, creativity and even a nice locality. No wonder I was constantly being disappointed. Now, in my portfolio existence, I could dismantle that package, do some things for money, other things for other reasons. She was a great egg packer. I had been a good teacher. I could and should use that talent to earn the money that I needed. I also realized that I should do it as well as I could for as much as I could reasonably charge, so that I could earn the money in as short a time as possible. She packed eggs only on Sundays. I would have to do a lot more paid work than that.

Elizabeth and I decided to allocate 150 days a year to paid work if I could get it, those days to include all the preparation, administration, marketing and travelling involved. At best I might have only fifty fee-earning days to support the rest of my life. They had better be good days, and profitable ones. We then put in twenty-five days for gift work, roughly 10 per cent of my paid working time, leaving ninety days for home work, holidays and leisure, in all of which I vowed to do my share.

'Ninety days for leisure,' a friend said. 'That's a nice lifestyle you have invented for yourselves.' We pointed out that most people expected a weekend off fifty-two times a year, plus eight public holidays and at least fifteen working days holiday a year – 127 days in total. Unlike most people, we had added together all our unallocated time. That was because we were proposing to divide our days as well as our work into chunks. No longer would we be bound by the traditional chunks of industrial society. We were free to re-chunk our lives in any way that we liked. We realized that if our work was based at home we would be tempted to work all day and every day, a 24/7 lifestyle. Instead we planned to try and take each Sunday off as a regular rule, leaving forty days for perhaps four ten-day holiday breaks.

'But you are only giving yourselves half a year to earn money,' was the reaction of another friend, when we explained our plans.

'We want to do as little paid work as possible,' we said, 'in order to leave the maximum amount of time for our other work. With luck half of our time on that sort of work will be enough.'

'Enough?' she exclaimed. 'How do you know what enough is? Surely you can never have too much?'

'I am nearly fifty years old,' I replied. 'At this stage in life, I can make a guess at how much money we will need to provide for our future. With luck the books may provide a little extra. There is no point in making more than we need.'

'I don't think you can ever have enough,' she said. 'If there is some left over you can always give it to your children or buy yourselves some luxury.'

'I don't believe in spoiling the children, but the real point is that if we spent more time making money we would have less time to do the things we really want to do, which is writing in my case and photography in Elizabeth's. We don't want to be slaves to money; in fact, the lower we can set our level of enough the more freedom we will have to do other things. Instead of setting you free, money can actually chain you to your paid work.'

She went away shaking her head, but the idea of an annual quota for our earnings has been the basis of our life ever since. I'm a cautious chap and I am careful to set the quota at a comfortable level, but one that I am fairly sure I can achieve within the allotted time. Income, too, has a portfolio element to it; it doesn't all come in one cheque for anyone. For some there are bits of a pension or maybe dividends from savings or inheritance. Money while you sleep, I call this. I had neither of these but I did secure an annual commitment to a part-time teaching role back at my old business school which was a reassuring chunk to start with. Then there were fees for occasional articles, small advance royalties for a new book, a few assignments to appear on company training programmes, an unexpected request to make that TV broadcast.

It all added up, just, although I was uncomfortably aware that I wasn't making much provision for our old age, or for the tax man. These things used to be deducted at source when I was in my organizations. Portfolio people have to remember that their income is now gross, not net. You are never as rich as you think you are. You will be pleased to know, my accountant told me, that when you are over sixty you can put 40 per cent of your income, tax free, into a pension scheme. Yes, but first you have to earn that extra 40 per cent, and there will still be 30 per cent or so to allow for tax, nowadays to be paid in advance. In other words I would eventually have to earn at least 70 per cent more than I needed to take advantage of that tax concession. So much for the joys of independence! Some comfort came from the fact that there were so many strings to my monetary bow. If any one of them broke, I would survive, none was crucial.

Nevertheless, the first years were full of that nervous back-of-the-envelope calculating. I was hitting the real dilemmas of the independent worker – how best to advertise one's availability and skills, and how much to charge for them. I had grown up in that vicarage where money wasn't mentioned and where advertising oneself would have been seen as a form of boasting. How did other independents do it, I wondered? Actors, for instance, or musicians, sports stars or fashion models? They all paid others to do the marketing for them, I realized, and indeed I already had an agent myself, but only for my writings which weren't, apparently, going to be worth much.

It was Elizabeth who, once again, came to my rescue. Annoyed by my willingness to go anywhere at any time, to speak or preach or teach – I was desperate at first – while often returning with nothing more to show for it than my rail fares and a token paperweight as a present, she appointed herself as my manager, insisting that she negotiated all assignments on my behalf in advance. In fact she actually wrote to the organizers of a couple of recent engagements apologizing for the fact that I had neglected to agree the fee and suggesting that payment by return would oblige. In each case it arrived, without demur. In my innocence of the world I had just entered I did not know that one could charge money for speaking at a business dinner. I soon learnt.

Uncontaminated by business schools, Elizabeth nevertheless knew instinctively what needed to be done. She would focus my paid work, she said, so that it was all part of a pattern, even though done for a wide range of assorted clients.

'You need to be a brand,' she said.

'Where did you pick up that sort of marketing jargon?' I asked. 'You must have been reading some of those business books.'

'It's just common sense. People need to know what you stand for, and what they are paying for when they ask you to speak or teach. I can only sell you if I am proud of what you do, if I feel that you are special in some way. OK, call it reputation, if you like, but you need to build one and then protect it.'

It sounded a bit weird, to make myself into a brand. But she was right. Portfolio people should not and cannot be all things to all people. They have to be special in some way if they are going to stand out in a crowded marketplace without huge expenditures in advertising or PR. To an independent, reputation, reputation, reputation is all there is.

Nevertheless some marketing is necessary. The world needs to know that you are available. Some newly-formed independents send out brochures, some distribute CVs to everyone they can think of. Others entertain potential clients in the hope that generous libations will bring their own rewards. It feels like scattering seed on rocks. We invited a whole range of friends and acquaintances to lunches, 'just to let you know that we have returned from that foreign country called Windsor Castle' we said, hoping that they would ask what I intended to do. Too often they assumed that I had retired, that word portfolio people learn to dread. 'Make sure that you get out of bed every morning,' one of them advised me. No hope there, I realized, of an offer of work.

But the wind of gossip does scatter some of those seeds more widely. Eventually the phone does ring, the letters of invitation do arrive, most of them, sadly, dreadfully unsuitable. 'Bad for your reputation,' advised Elizabeth, turning them down before I could protest. It was not easy to look at those potential gift horses in the mouth and send them away. But she was right, you shape your own reputation.

Then I got lucky. If you write a book the publishers require you to publicize it, with interviews and features that they arrange. In the process you inevitably publicize yourself and your brand. Whichever way you choose to do it, it seems to take about two years for the results to show, because in the end it is only word of mouth and a string of satisfied clients or successful projects that count. It is another way of sowing seeds for the future – and waiting.

I call it luck, but we are often the authors of our own luck. Apples fall unpredictably into our laps, I used to tell my students, but it is more likely to happen if you go and stand in the orchard and give the tree the odd shake. Publishers don't often invite you to write books; you have to write them first, even publish them yourself if need be, as Elizabeth did for her first two photographic books. Do that and you are in the orchard.

My particular paid work portfolio is unusual. It is designed to fit the few things that I can do. Its details, or time allocations, cannot be a precise model for anyone else, because every portfolio life is different. That is the charm of the idea. Many ex-executives do successfully turn themselves into consultants of one sort or another. Others put together a portfolio of non-executive directorships. Some, those with surplus funds, invest in small start-up companies where their experience is as much help as their money. Our own children chose to be portfolio people from the start, willy-nilly in the case of our actor son who knew that acting would seldom provide for all his needs, but through deliberate planning in the case of our osteopath daughter who wants a diversified life and restricts her osteopathy workload to three days a week in order to leave room for other forms of creative activity, another way to chunk her work and her life.

Portfolio living may be a new concept for organization man or woman, but it would be no news at all to those who have never worked in organizations. There are more of these than we think, because they are often disguised as organizations rather than self-employed. Over 60 per cent of all the registered businesses in Britain have no employees, only the owner. Some of these business fleas go on to be serious alchemists, building new organizations of their own. Most don't; they are portfolio people masquerading as businesses. John Smith Associates often turns out to be just John Smith.

Then there are all the small farmers, artisans and craftspeople, furniture restorers, minicab drivers, photographers, bread-and-breakfast providers, odd-job men and gardeners, the growing army of the self-employed who have never heard of fancy concepts like portfolio living. But they all know that money comes in different bundles from different sources, that we are each responsible for our own destiny, that no one person or organization can or should own us. They understand, too, that their time is theirs to manage, even if they don't manage it too well, that enough is as good as a feast, even if they never quantify that notion, and that reputation is critical to future work

– all concepts central to portfolio thinking and to the life of a flea.

Not all independents are there by choice. Often, as organizations slim down their payrolls, it is an alternative that they would have preferred had not come their way. For the truth is that a portfolio life is not all roses, even when it works well. Winston Fletcher, an advertising executive turned successful portfolio person, with a mix of paid work and gift work, of consultancy and non-executive directorships, puts it well: 'Portfolio people are hired for themselves alone. This is deliciously flattering, but means that you can't call substitutes onto the pitch. You have to be at every game yourself – well prepared and fighting fit . . . Compared with working in an organization, it's a mildly lonely life. Portfolio life means forever scurrying hither and thither . . . you have little control over the date or time of meetings . . . Portfolio employers do not, by and large, provide offices or secretaries. In these days of laptops, e-mails and faxes you might think such privations would not matter. They do.' Most of all, he says, to those used to executive positions in organizations, is the swap of power for influence. 'You are not responsible for running any of the shows in which you appear . . . It is all a tad insubstantial. Portfolio jobs provide lots of opportunities for pride but few for ambition.'

You do not have to build a portfolio of mainly advisory work, as Winston Fletcher has done. But he is right in emphasizing that portfolio people are seldom in a position to run any sizeable organization. We do trade power for influence. Personally I found that a great relief and, as Fletcher says, often very flattering. No longer did I lie awake at night worrying that I had delegated the wrong things to the wrong person, that I wouldn't fill my course quotas or meet the budget, even that the ancient buildings we used in Windsor Castle might catch fire from someone's careless cigarette. On the other hand when I was invited to speak to some gathering of the great and occasionally good I knew it was because of who I was and not what I was.

The most flattering thing of all, however, for those who have traded power for influence, is to find an idea that you have tossed out into the ether picked up and used by people whom you have never met. I once got a letter from the other side of the world, with no address so I couldn't reply. All it said was, 'Thank you for your books. They gave me hope and changed my life.' To me that letter was worth more than rubies. Never underestimate the effect of influence. In any list of the most significant people of the last century the names of such as Sigmund Freud, Albert Einstein and, more recently, Tim Berners-Lee who gave us the world wide web must surely figure, people of no power but with an influence on the way we think and live that will still be there when we have long forgotten the men and women of power, the Hitlers, the Churchills and the Stalins. The person chosen by the British people as the hero of the last millennium was William Shakespeare, a man who commanded nothing except words.

Alas, all is not sugar and honey. There is too, the odd insulting letter, the feedback from the conference that the organizers so considerately send on to you, in which someone has called your contribution 'a load of old rubbish' or what one person eloquently called 'a long paean of self-congratulation'. And, if you are brave enough to expose your thoughts by writing books, there are the reviews. Oh, those reviews! All authors, actors and other performers claim not to read them. They all do, with bated breath, ignoring the favourable phrases but committing to unforgiving memory every piece of criticism, uneasily aware that it is possibly all too accurate. All reviews are good reviews, the publisher says, it all means that you have been noticed, but they don't have to read them.

One early book of mine received a scathing review from *The Economist*. I rang my publisher in some distress.

'What are you talking about?' she said, 'There was a photograph beside the review, that's almost unknown for that magazine, it's brilliant.' I was unconvinced. And I can still quote, word for word, the acerbic comments of one of my critics ten years ago. It was a review in the *Accountantsí Journal* in Ireland, not the world's most widely read magazine, but that didn't matter to me. The chap had found my Achilles' heel. By way of a cure, Elizabeth arranged for me to meet him in a Dublin pub.

'You should see the original that I wrote, the one the lawyers wouldn't let through,' he said by way of greeting, producing the script from his pocket. He turned out to be a frustrated author himself, angry that I should have had my obviously lesser work published when he hadn't. One spectre had been killed, but there have been many others down the years.

The hard fact is that those who live by their own swords lay themselves open to wounds as well as flattery. An independent's life, the life of the so-called 'freelance' (originally a free lance in wars), has to be an exposed one. It does require self-belief, a willingness to learn from feedback even when it comes in the form of criticism or even abuse, and the acceptance that the sensitivity necessary to understand the clients' needs probably also means a thin skin, easily bruised and slow to heal. Nothing in life is without its costs, but, as I have experienced it, the freedom that comes from portfolio work more than compensates for the hurts.

For all that I celebrate its advantages, it can be a daunting prospect at the start. Not only do you need a saleable skill, you also need to be able to sell it and price it, or to have someone to do that for you. Much of portfolio working is indeed lonely, although my version of it is more a succession of short-term close relationships, like shipboard friendships, intense while they last, soon forgotten when the next ship comes along. Then again, I am fortunate – I live with my agent and manager which not only fights the loneliness but keeps the agency fees within the family.

Nevertheless, more and more of us will have to face up to this sort of lifestyle at some time or other. Organizations, whether in business or not, will continue to cut back their core commitments whilst simultaneously increasing their range and scope. They will cover the gap by contracting-in the services and expertise that they need, much of it from professional service firms but much, too, from individuals. Those cores themselves will need younger people, people who are prepared to put in the hours and the miles that global and 24-hour operations now require. There may still be a need for a few greybeards but not for many. More organizations will have an age profile like the army – a pyramid with a large base of the young and eager, rapidly narrowing to the few wise guys at the top – and, like the army, the organization will be the first career for many, the prelude to life as a flea.

It is a life that for many will be cushioned at its start either by an early pension or by a contract to do as an independent what used to be done as an employee. It is also a life in which retirement will seldom figure. For portfolio people there is no finite cut-off date when work stops, only subtle changes in the mix of the portfolio, less paid work, more of the other varieties. When you ask an ageing portfolio person what they do, they will still take a paragraph to answer you. Even if most of their income now comes from pensions or savings they won't think of themselves as retired, any more than I have ever heard a woman call herself retired – for her there was always work to be done, somewhere.

That I believe to be the good news; I have always seen retirement as giving up on life. The bad news is that independence encourages selfishness. Our loyalty, as fleas, is first to ourselves and our future, secondly to our current project, team or group and only thirdly to an organization, a community or, sometimes, to our family. Yet without commitment there is no responsibility for others and without responsibility no care.

The real challenge of fleadom is the looming threat of the selfish society. That is the focus of my final chapter. It is a challenge to which I have no answer, only some hopes. Here I have tried to describe how I myself took the leap into an independent existence. After a difficult start it has worked wonderfully, in the sense that my life really became exciting as I approached the age of sixty. It was a long time to wait, but worth it. I can only encourage others to try it and to persevere, to find their own formula and their own mix, to move away from what they are not, until they discover what it is that they can uniquely do, to be content with influence and its special delights, and to make do with enough in order to be free.

9

CHUNKING OUR LIVES

It took ten years for my working life to take off.

My literary agent sold my fourth book to a new publisher and a new editor. It was a different sort of book this time, written not for academics or students or even for managers, but for the general reader. Authors always hate letting their work loose on the public, but I was more than usually nervous about this one which was called *Changing*. It laid out a picture of a very different world of work from the one we were used to, a world in which many of the things we took for granted were likely to be turned on their heads. I wasn't sure that I could make it convincing, or that I could write for the general public. The editor took it away to read over the weekend and to show it to some colleagues.

She phoned me on Tuesday. 'We think you should call it *The Age of Unreason*,' she said.

'That's a great title,' I replied, a little startled, 'but there's nothing in the book about unreason.'

'Put it in,' she said. 'If you think about it, the whole book is asking people to think unreasonably. Oh, and it lacks a proper ending.'

Then I remembered that great quote from Bernard Shaw about all change coming from unreasonable men, because the reasonable ones expect the world to go on much as it always has. I put it in, added a rather emotional and personal conclusion, and changed the title. I suspect that the title made all the difference. Who, in retrospect, would have bothered to look at a book called *Changing*?

The editor was Gail Rebuck, now the chairman of Random House and still, I am glad to say, my publisher. She has taught me that one should never be too proud or too sensitive to accept advice, even criticism, particularly from those who are on your side. We are seldom the best judges of our own work. Authors are lucky people – they have editors, and editors are accomplices, allies not competitors. I still flinch, of course, when my work comes back with phrases altered, paragraphs crossed out and question marks against my favoured bits, but it is still my responsibility to accept or reject the suggested changes and I know, deep down, that they are all intended to make the work better. To have a friendly critic who shares your hopes and ambitions is, I have come to understand, a huge privilege.

That book sold well. More importantly, it was published in America, with the support of another visionary publisher, Carol Franco, who was busy building up the Harvard Business School Press. This was 1989. Americans had scant respect for anything akin to management or business thinking that came from Europe, which they saw as an economic basket case. Few if any European management writers had been published there at that time. For me it was a breakthrough. Suddenly I was known beyond British shores as other countries felt bold enough to follow the Americans and publish their own editions. I was profiled in *Fortune* magazine. Invitations to speak hither and yon started to arrive. It was tempting to get big-headed and to forget our rule of enough. 'Nothing in Excess,' I recalled in time, had been another of those inscriptions in the temple of Apollo at Delphi.

It was tempting, too, to forget that Elizabeth had her own ambitions. 'I'm very happy for you,' she said one day, 'but I am now completely submerged in your life. I have no time or place of my own. My passion is photography and I want to be able to practise it.'

For the past five years she had been studying for a degree in photography one day a week at the University of Westminster and had just heard that she had passed with honours. It was time to remember another set of my theories, ones that I had only recently set down in that book that was selling around the world, but which I was ignoring in my own home. Success can spoil you, if you aren't careful.

The theories stemmed from research that I had conducted back at the London Business School twenty years earlier. Those were the days when executive stress was not yet an idea whose time had come. Nevertheless, as I looked at the conflict in my own life at the time between the pressures of work and the demands of my family, I wondered if I could discover any clues to the elusive balance of work and marriage. Maybe, I thought, I could find some magic formula which would not only help me but might be the basis for at least an article, maybe a book. Publish or perish is the old academic formula and I had still, at that time, published nothing.

I had a group ready to hand for my research. They were the executives who had been on the management courses that I had created and run for the previous three years. Many of them lived and worked in or near London and might be available for interview. Most were in their mid-thirties, married with two or three young children. Twenty-three of them agreed to take part in the research. That meant both husband and wife completing an attitude survey (with the impressive name of the Edwards Personal Preference Schedule) and meeting my research assistant, an American graduate psychologist called Pam Berger, for a long interview.

Of course, no way could such a hopelessly biased and inadequate sample be called anything other than a pilot study. It was also a child of its time. Even calling it a study of marriage patterns dates it, for the year was 1972. The executives were, to begin with, all male, and inescapably middle class. They were all happily married, for the first and, they assumed, the only time – or they would never have agreed to participate; they were all British and all moderately successful in either business, government or the voluntary sector. Nevertheless I hoped that the study would come up with some pointers, some clues to managing the mix of home and work that I could test out in later and broader research. I might even, I thought in my more secret dreams, make my name if I could come up with a neat formula for marital success in the business world.

That didn't happen, of course. Life is neither so predictable nor so manageable. What we did discover were some distinct marriage patterns, or what I would now call a variety of options for relationships.

The survey is described in some detail in *The Age of Unreason*. We grouped the individuals in four boxes according to their key scores on the questionnaires, scores that revealed their unconscious priorities, a desire for achievement or for autonomy, perhaps, or a need to care and support rather than to dominate.

We lettered the boxes A to D and put names on them to indicate the mix of priorities that they represented. The B box we called Thrusting, because it combined high needs for what the attitude survey called Achievement as well as Autonomy, whereas the A box we called Involved, being a mix of Achievement and Caring. D was all Caring and C all Autonomy, so we called it the Loner box. That produced the simplified diagram shown on the next page.

We then joined up each couple and their boxes and gave the mixes neutral names, such as AA or BD. We ended up with four different combinations, out of a theoretically possible sixteen. That was all done from the numbers on the questionnaire. The interesting part came next, when we compared our observations of how they differed in the way they related to each other and organized their lives.

Achievement

A Involved	B Thrusting
D Caring	C Loners

Caring   Autonomy

The dominant pattern was BD, what might be called the Traditional Marriage (he was B, a high achiever who valued autonomy, and she was D, a Carer). In this pattern the husband's work was the defining core, around which all else revolved. The wife was in a supportive and caring role, and happy with it, responsible for all that went on in the home, including the upbringing of the children, leaving the husband free to concentrate on his career.

There was one instance of a Competitive Marriage (BB), a union of two Thrusters, in which both partners were high achievers but with high scores, too, on Autonomy. They had similar full-time jobs and no children. They lived what we described as a low-slung life, with sports cars and a modern apartment, eating out rather than in, two incomes to splash about, competing with each other in a friendly rivalry, working hard and playing hard but with largely separate daytime lives.

There was also a Segregated Marriage (CC), of two loners

who had both scored high on Autonomy but low on everything else. They managed to live together and bring up children without sharing either time or space. When one came home from work the other went out. Everyone in the house had their own space. There were no tables or chairs where a communal meal might take place. Each member of the family, including the young children, was responsible for preparing their own food and for their own entertainment.

The other principal marriage pattern, however, was the Shared Marriage (AA), one in which all roles were shared. Both partners had scored high in the questionnaire on both the Achievement and Caring dimensions. Both partners therefore worked, but both also cooked and looked after the children as and when needed. Whereas the Traditional Marriage tended to live in homes with designated rooms (dining, sitting, study, kitchen etc.), the Shared Marriage homes were open space, dominated by an untidy family kitchen where everything seemed to happen.

Nothing too surprising, perhaps, in all of this. They all claimed to be happy and we have all seen examples of each pattern among our friends. But then we started to talk about the study to other groups.

'You have only taken a snapshot in time,' some said. 'It would be interesting to know whether these patterns remain constant over a longer period.'

'That's right,' said others. 'Many marriages start off as equal partnerships, rather like your so-called competitive marriage, but inevitably things change when the kids come along. Someone has to look after them, just at the moment when careers are taking off. Usually it's the woman who stays at home, falling into the traditional marriage pattern as long as the kids are young.'

'Not necessarily for ever,' said others. 'As soon as the children were a bit older, we moved into a shared marriage pattern, both of us contributing jobs and home care.'

'We tried that,' said another, 'but it was very stressful. I had to turn down a promotion because it would have meant moving to another part of the country, bad news for my partner and the children who would have had to move jobs and schools. You can't be too ambitious and still share the home care.'

'Your patterns describe my life,' said an older man. 'We started off idealistically as a shared marriage, then I got promoted and two children arrived so we changed to a traditional marriage pattern and my wife gave up her job. When the kids grew up, she started work again and for a while we enjoyed the fast life of your competitive marriage, but that soon degenerated into your segregated pattern and last year we got divorced.'

People do indeed move through the patterns. Ten years after doing the study I bumped into Richard, the male half of the one competitive marriage in our sample. He had put on weight and was expensively dressed, clearly doing well.

'How is Judy?' I asked, half expecting to hear that she was no longer around.

'Oh, she's fine,' he said. 'We live down in the country now, with the two kids. She's into roses in a big way.'

They had obviously moved into the traditional pattern and were seemingly content.

Maybe, I reflected, the secret of a continuing relationship is to be able to change patterns as life's cycle moves on. Many friends and colleagues, I was noticing, had not been able to adjust when the need for a traditional marriage pattern had ended with the departure of the children. Suddenly there was no common bond to hold the two together, with no children around to manage and the parents dead or parked in a home. Their two separate lives now seemed to exist in two separate worlds, each with its own groups of friends and its own interests.

Sometimes they struggled on together, in a version of the segregated pattern, for the sake of the children, they said, or out of habit. Often, however, one or other found a new partner in order to start a new pattern. One friend married a work colleague and, much to the amazement of those who knew him, was to be discovered cooking and serving the meals in a new loft-type home, delighting in the shared pattern of their lives.

Conversely, another male friend, who had adapted to the

caring role in their traditional pattern while his wife worked in the limelight, suddenly took off, to live much more modestly with a new partner. 'I felt trapped in my role,' he said. 'I wanted to share my life with someone who shared more of my own interests.'

Elizabeth and I have female friends who have done the same, changing partners in order to change patterns, but I resolved that in my new life we would be different. Divorce or separation were not in the vicarage tradition. Besides, we still loved each other, I hoped. I had thought and assumed that we were a partnership with a shared pattern to our marriage. Unconsciously, however, we had slipped into a variation on the traditional pattern. The children were no longer at home for Elizabeth to care for, but she was still caring for me, at the sacrifice of her own work and interests.

We had to make some choices.

'You could get yourself a secretary,' she said, 'and join one of those speakers' bureaux, they will find you plenty of work – which you will need if you have to pay the secretary's salary. Then I would be free to concentrate on my photography.'

I recalled my research of all those years ago. What she was suggesting would lead to a segregated marriage. I loved her too much and my work too little for that to be an option. I also needed her for my work, for her intuitions, her wise critiques, her insistence that we keep to our work mix, her ability to market my wares and organize our travels. I would need a whole platoon of talents to compensate and even then it would not be the same. There had to be another option.

There was no straightforward solution, alas, in the models from my research. She could not do her work while she was organizing mine. We had to find a way to free her up, to give her time for both. Perhaps, I reflected, there were other ways of combining those patterns than the ones my original sample had used. Could we, I wondered, invent our own variant of the shared marriage? Eventually, we decided to split the year, and to lay another matrix on top of our work mix.

I agreed to do all my paid work and gift work in the six winter months. The summer months would be hers. They would also be available for my study work, the reading and writing that were the materials for my published work. During her six months I would lend her what assistance I could. I was not a photographer but I could fetch and carry, hold umbrellas to ward off sun or showers, act as chauffeur or companion on her engagements and, more usefully perhaps, be her wordsmith for the photographic books that were one output of her work. It cannot be as tidy a division as it sounds. There will always be some advance planning for my work that has to be done in her six months, and there is always some work on her books that overruns into my months. There is also the odd exception to prove the rule; no point in punishing ourselves when we both agree that the exception is worthwhile.

That divided up the work. I started explaining to any would-be clients that the summer months were my closed season, devoted to study, and hoped that they would return at another season. Not all of them understood. I had to accept that. Elizabeth's excuse was more acceptable, that there was not enough natural light in the winter for her style of photography. But not all her clients were prepared to wait six months for their engagement photograph or for that special Christmas portrait. We both discovered that it requires some strength of mind to say 'No' to pleading clients, and at the beginning we made more exceptions than we should have.

That still left the home work. There were no children left at home to look after, nor parents alive to care for, but we both worked at home all day, received clients, held meetings at home most days, entertained our friends at home. That meant housework and cooking. We split our life between London and the country, where we do our creative work. We spend roughly equal time in each, so we agreed that we would each be responsible for the cooking, catering and housekeeping in one home. I chose the country, partly because cooking is a wonderful antidote to the purely cerebral activity of reading and writing. Elizabeth was happy with the town flat for her share of the home work, which left her all the hours in the country to concentrate on her photography with minimal distraction.

It is a very contrived way of life, and one with unanticipated consequences. For one thing, we are seldom out of each other's sight or sound. At one conference a management consultant rather patronizingly consoled Elizabeth for her patience in being married to someone who, he assumed, lived his own sort of itinerant life.

'I admire the way you wives put up with our absences,' he said. 'Tell me, what is the longest time your husband is away for?'

Elizabeth smiled sweetly. 'About fifty minutes, while he is down at the supermarket.'

We like it that way, to many people's surprise. The old adage that she married him for life but not for lunch does not hold for us. Maybe we are both reverting to our beginnings. My father was home for lunch in the vicarage every day. Elizabeth's father, an army officer in garrison towns, was also home by late morning most days. In my youth in the Irish countryside I knew no one who wasn't home for lunch. Even the shopkeepers and the solicitors lived above their work.

We also like the fact that we each know all the people that the other knows. There are very few private friendships or contacts in our new life, no room for secret lovers or boozy football chums. Like Siamese twins, you have to take us both together in almost every aspect of our lives.

It is our version of a shared pattern of marriage. Yet it is also, for much of the day, a segregated pattern. We work separately, in separate rooms, performing separate functions. We are different personalities with different habits. You only have to look at our two work spaces to see that there is no way that we could work in the same room, nor even share the same kitchen. Such a life is not without its strains, of course. Togetherness requires a tolerance for difference, and tolerance, I fear, isn't always on offer if one of us blunders or forgets.

Our life is very different now from our first twenty-five years together. I sometimes think that we are on our second marriage, with all its new discoveries of each other. The difference is that it is a marriage of the same people. There is no dispute, therefore, in our second marriage, over who gets the old photo albums, or the house. I used to be two separate people, at work and at home, and was never sure which was more truly me. Now I have no choice. I felt deprived at first, but then relieved.

Our way of chunking our life is not for everyone. Few people, for one thing, could divide their work portfolio so neatly into two parts. For partners both to be able to do it must be almost unique. Few couples, too, would find that their talents so neatly fit together, so that each can serve the other. The timing has to be right, as well. We could not have done it earlier in our lives, while children were around and there were mortgages and more bills to be paid.

For many, it sounds too cosy to be real, living in each other's pockets come rain, come sun, come day, come night. Most people want more of that space to be themselves. I would not have believed it to be possible myself. I describe it in order to illustrate the lengths to which one can go in reinventing the way that independent fleas can live, sometimes have to live. Many already find their own patterns. Think of actors, sports people, doctors, architects, consultants, all of whom often marry someone of the same profession, but who seldom work in the same place at the same time. More of us will, I have argued, be leading actors' lives and, with them, actors' marriages. There are other mixes of the shared and segregated patterns. Some couples manage to live in two different cities, countries or even continents. They meet for chunks of time, moving into each other's space for a weekend, a month or two months at a time, switching roles as they do. They say that the intensity of their chunks together more than compensates for their times apart. Besides, they say, they are freer to concentrate on their work chunks when they are apart.

Chunks, in fact, become essential to anyone who wants to keep control of their life. The old chunks of the agricultural age, Sundays and festivals, were followed by the more secular chunks of the industrial age – weekends, bank holidays and, eventually, annual holidays. The modern information and global age brings new pressures. Somewhere the world is always awake and working, even on 25 December, which was once the day that at least the Christian world stood still. Now it's only the British railways that stop moving. The 24/7 week is no longer something confined to hospitals and hotels, who have always known it. Statutory holiday breaks get longer but mobile phones and e-mail mean that the work follows you to the beach or the swimming pool.

I once attended the launch of the formal Vision and Values statement of a major international company at a gathering of the top thirty managers. The statement was the company's attempt to set down in writing the principles that would guide all its policies. Item six declared that the firm actively encouraged a proper balance between work and family. A hand was raised.

'Then why,' the person behind the hand asked, 'are we meeting here on a Sunday?'

'Because it's the only day that we were all available,' replied the Chief Executive.

Good intentions give way to hard reality in most organizations – and in the life of a flea.

However much we shut the doors of our work places in the evenings, and usually on Sundays, it is hard not to creep back in when deadlines press, or a new idea strikes. Work can be exciting, more sexy at times than any alternative on offer. In the early days of the new London Business School it was often hard to tear myself away from the eager students who had paid good money and, flatteringly, wanted every ounce of knowledge or supposed wisdom that they could suck out of the faculty. Organizations have tried locking their offices at night and weekends to keep their people from working too hard, only to find that information leaps all fences these days, as people went on working on their home computers, phones and faxes.

The French are making a brave attempt to defy the 24/7 week with their law restricting it to thirty-five hours. It is a move widely welcomed by the hourly-paid workers who, almost unanimously, say that it gives them more time with their families or to enjoy their leisure. But organizations still have to work the same hours as before, so the thirty-five hours have been averaged out over the year, allowing the organizations to adjust the hours to their needs, and, in some cases to the needs of the individual workers. Productivity in France has actually increased, partly as a result, and some more jobs have been created, but, although I have no statistical evidence to support the anecdotes, one has to suspect that the hours of those responsible for implementing the new flexibility have increased, whether they are worked in the office or at home.

The flexibility that the new law requires of organizations will, in time, force more and more workers into a form of self-employment, even if they aren't tempted to use some of their new free time to earn more money by more work. It will also encourage organizations to go down the portfolio route as a way of making the law work for them. Paradoxically, France may become a land of workaholic fleas.

The old chunks of work and non-work don't function any more. We have to invent new chunks. What will be new in the years ahead, I believe, is that portfolio thinking will enter the world inside the organization. The signs are there in the increased emphasis on what people are calling work/life balance – as if the two were separate concepts – in the legislation that makes more parental leave available to both sexes and the increasing readiness of organizations to provide sabbatical leave to those they would hate to lose, but most of all in the disillusionment felt by many who find that they have traded their freedom for bundles of bonuses or stock options.

In order to retain and to entice the next generation of talent, organizations will find themselves allowing their key people to build their own mixed portfolios, which may include guaranteed time for home work at particular points in the family life cycle, periods of study work of one sort or another, opportunities for gift work in the local community and even a mix of different bits of paid work within the organization. Those organizations who have established their own Internet subsidiaries or their internal venture capital initiatives have often been influenced as much by the need to convince their employees that they aren't just staid, fuddy-duddy stalwarts as by the genuine need to create new futures for themselves.

Already research is establishing that those subsets of portfolio life, flexible working and job-sharing, the latter mostly used by women, are resulting in improved productivity and job satisfaction. BT in Britain views flexible working as important to the retention of talent in some of their divisions. The elephants need fleas, and fleas like to control their own lives and build their own portfolios. If they can do so under the umbrella of the organization so much the better, they will avoid most of the downsides of a portfolio life on the outside.

As organizations loosen up their work arrangements, so we are freed to define our own chunks in our life. We should use that freedom, even at the cost of some loss of income, to rebalance our mix of work. Life's priorities often look different when you get to the other end, when you often wish you had done things differently. But we could try to be wise before our time. Amyarta Sen, the Nobel prizewinnng economist, has insisted that wealth is not to be measured by what we have but by what we can do. Chunking is our chance to grow richer by Sen's definition.

10

LAST THOUGHTS

I have been celebrating the independent life because I believe it to be the likely future for many of us, not because I believe it to be the ideal for all.

If I am honest, the thought of a world populated only by fleas, of independents and small organizations, fills me with dread. If the other side of freedom's coin is aloneness then the obverse of independence is selfishness, for living up to the possibilities within yourself can mean ignoring the possibilities in anyone else. Business, said Randy Komisar in his book on life in Silicon Valley, *The Monk and the Riddle*, asks only two things of people, to be aggressive and to be greedy. In 1999 the Pope expressed his own fears about what he called neo-liberalism: 'Based on a purely economic concept of man, this system considers profit and the law of the market as its only parameters, to the detriment of the dignity and the respect due to individuals and people.'

Thank God, then, for the best of the elephants, I find myself saying, for the employment organizations and the instruments of government. For all their limitations they do bind us together and force us to compromise our freedoms for the sake of a common cause, or, in the case of government, for the needs of others. James Madison, one of the founders of American democracy, once said that the frailties of mankind are the best basis for good government. Government is there to mitigate our failures, our failures to look after both ourselves and our neighbours.

In the past we relied on communities of one sort or another to take up some of the burden. But those communities, the work organization, the family and the neighbourhood, are changing before our eyes. Most of us used to belong to all three, with the rights and the responsibilities that stemmed from our member-ship. Now we want the rights and the pleasures but without the responsibilities. I am as bad as anyone. I like the anonymity of cities, because it imposes no obligations on me.

On the other hand, I half envy those who live in tight communities, whose friends all know each other, who have formal roles in the community, who will be missed by many when they die or leave. I can even begin to understand why people will risk their lives fighting to preserve a tribal community in the Balkans and elsewhere. Their commitment is repaid by a sense that they belong and that they matter. On a personal level, our own neighbours, I suspect, would neither know nor care too much were we to disappear from their midst.

I am probably not that unusual these days. I am reluctant to mortgage my time. Others go further. They see a long-term commitment to anyone or anything as mortgaging their whole future, as limiting the choices that might otherwise have been on offer. 'I think you have a problem with commitment,' said my young cousin to her lover when he refused to marry her. To sit loose and fancy-free is the preferred option of many, both young and old, while to be loyal to partner or company is seen as an irrational attachment that gets in the way of ambition and efficiency.

Lifetime employment is neither offered nor desired. Both parties want to keep their options open. 'Till death us do part', the vow I made on my wedding day, is seen by many as a romantic but unrealistic ideal, and by others as just silly. Neither of our children is 'in a relationship' as the modern phrase has it. They are part of a growing band of singletons by choice. Should they decide to marry, then pre-nuptial agreements, which assume the end of a relationship, are becoming more common. 'Friends are for life,' a young woman informed me, 'relationships come and go.' We talk of women having a child 'by so and so' rather as we speak of the sires of racehorses. 'Relationship churn' it is called, new jargon for new times. Commitment has been truncated in favour of choice.

As a result, many families are now often spliced together rather than grown, full of stepfathers and half-sisters and the like. However well the new extended families work the implied message must be there – that choice is more important than commitment. More and more women and men avoid the dilemma by choosing not to have children at all in order to retain their independence; indeed, the decline in the birthrate through-out the developed world must be one of the more surprising outcomes of the fashion for the independent life of a flea. If the poorer half of the world leapfrogs over the economy of the elephants and opts for more flea-type work and life, we may even see the world population start to decline.

Families, however, despite their many changes, at least show no signs of becoming virtual, unlike other communities. The Internet, for instance, offers virtual neighbourhoods and virtual work networks free for all. These can often start, or reinforce, real friendships and real work, but for those who want less commitment they also offer the possibility of friendships without responsibility, of communication without obligation. Fun they may be, these virtual communities, but they create only the illusion of intimacy and a pretence of community. A friend was amazed, he told me, to find that he now had seven hundred names on his e-mail address file. 'I need never be lonely now,' he said. But a mailing list is a long way from a tribe of friends or a hunting pack.

Should we be worried by the fact that more of us don't belong to any formal community? Probably. Life without belonging properly to anything, life without commitment, means life without responsibility to others or for others. The independent life is an invitation to selfishness and a recipe for a very privatized society. But where there is no responsibility for others there is no need for concepts of right or wrong. A world of independent fleas and small enterprises can become an amoral world. Do whatever you want, as long as it's within the law or, more realistically, as long as you don't get caught. Maximize your own advantage. Why not? What else could be more important?

The problem is that if we work on that basis we must assume that others will do so too. Trust is folly in this sort of world. Every agreement needs to be in writing and legally enforceable. Lawyers will have a field day, but the courts won't be able to cope with the flood of cases. Physically, life would become more dangerous as violence becomes more common, perhaps even more legitimate, in a society where everyone has to look after themselves. Houses become gated prisons, we arm ourselves when we venture forth, if not with guns, then with sprays and alarms. We discharge any lingering responsibility to others by paying our taxes and letting the government take care of their problems.

Bob Tyrrell, one of Britain's best analysts of social trends, describes this sort of world as one of 'competitive individualism'. In one scenario he can envisage the balance of power swinging to the individual and away from the corporation, with individuals advertising their availability on the Internet and inviting bids for their time. Doctors and teachers, for example, would be independent or in small partnerships, hired in by hospitals and schools. It would be an age of hyperactivity with work and recreation being available around the clock, many choosing to play or work at unsocial hours because of the discount or premiums on offer. We would define ourselves more by what we buy and how we choose to live, by our lifestyle, than by where we work or have our home. The stereotype of the

American attitude – the harder I work the more I can buy – would trump the European idea that work is only a part of life.

The signs of this sort of world are already there, a world that seems to be designed for the successful flea, a winner-take-all world. Domestic service has even been reinvented to look after the needs of the winners: there is a growing army of personal service providers, ranging from cooks, nannies and gardeners to holistic healers, personal trainers and personal shoppers who make life tolerable for the successful ones. The sting in this particular tail, however, is that these occupations, too, are for independent fleas, not employees.

The result is a growing gap between those who revel in this unequal and more separate world and those who can't cope. Government responds by trying to equip more people with the skills and qualifications to compete, but, however laudable their efforts, this may be a race where late starters can't catch up – unless they have the rare good fortune to find someone who plants a golden seed in them; unless they start to dream and go on to find a passion. I found it difficult enough to get started on an independent life, but at least I had had long years of apprenticeship in those elephants. How much harder it must be for someone leaving school with no organizations to practise in.

It is a world that I recognize and have participated in, even while I shudder at its implications. I can see why people advocate the return of the local community, why they go on about the responsibilities that go with rights and entitlements. I can understand why they should want to persuade themselves that most of us will end up as loyal long-term employees in stable organizations when we settle down, even if we experiment a bit in our twenties, and will twist the statistics to reassure themselves that the world isn't really changing, when most people know that it is.

There is, however, another possibility: the world could change differently.

Instead of a competitive individualism it could be a time of varied individualism. We may decide to be different from, rather than better than, our fellows. It could be a case of all-get-to-win rather than one-winner-get-all. We could choose to decide on our own definition of what winning might mean for us. Diversity might come to mean a variety of lifestyles, all acceptable, rather than a variety of races.

Bob Tyrrell, in another of his scenarios for the future, can foresee a society that values difference, in which live-and-let-live would be the new philosophy. Business is acknowledged for what it does, but other parts of life operate by another tempo and according to equally legitimate sets of values. Volunteering, public service and, he suggests, even religious devotion might regain their esteem. Pressure groups, from Greenpeace to Age Concern, will gain political legitimacy, as a more effective way to influence governments than a five-yearly vote.

The truth is that we shall probably see a bit of both scenarios, both competitive and varied individualism. Competitive individualism suits the young and the ambitious, it is the fuel that drives innovation and creativity, that builds businesses and forces institutions to change in tune with the times. A country or a business without this sort of energy withers. But not everyone enjoys the rat race that results, particularly as they get older.

With ambition spent by my middle years – been there, done that, or more truthfully tried that and failed that – I found that I wanted to change my priorities in life, moving to a slower, gentler pace with more time for contemplation, friendships and reflective work, with fewer deadlines and demands. It wasn't retirement that I wanted, but a rechunking of my life to leave more space for other things. The formula that my wife and I arrived at is peculiar to us, of course, but as the demographic profile of our society changes there are going to be many more healthy, vigorous middle-aged people around with the self-confidence to set their own priorities for the next stage of their lives and to chunk their lives in different ways. This may coincide with the growing trend for governments of all persuasions to encourage their citizens to take more responsibility for their own destinies. In any case, without organizations to employ and protect them, or without adequate support from the state, the new middle-aged will have to make their own choices and arrangements whether they feel up to it or not.

On the other hand, they will have votes, more votes than any other age group. Will they use that voting power for selfish ends, opting for whichever party offers ever higher pensions and subsidies to be paid for by the next generation, or will they press for more local control of local issues and less one-suit-fits-all solutions, for quieter streets and airplanes, cleaner air and greener organizations? Are the new middle-aged the true 'Trustees of our Future' that ambassador Kingman Brewster spoke of twenty years ago? The hope must be that they will live up to the challenge, even if it be only by using their votes for the good of the whole, not just for themselves.

This group will find that their combined purchasing power will set new fashions. The prediction is that they will increasingly buy time and service, not things. Health, tourism, education and personal services are tipped as the growth areas of the future. These are high touch rather than high tech businesses, even though technology will play a supportive role, and might herald a more personal, more friendly world of commerce. Who knows, they might even persuade offices to put real people at the end of those phone lines. Staying with the optimistic view, this group could choose to use their new consumer power to influence the behaviour of the corporate elephants, boycotting exploitative concerns and favouring environmentally virtuous ones.

There will also be more opportunity for individuals to make a difference in organizations, should they want to. That is because the unit of operation will everywhere get smaller and more accessible, even while the combinations get bigger. Government, for a start, will inevitably federalize, even though the British will not call it that, because of their visceral distrust of the term. More decisions will have to be taken locally and more finance raised locally, in recognition of the diversity of regions. In Europe the nation state will be squeezed between the pressures for harmonization through Brussels and the need for more of that regional diversity. Subsidiarity, the principle at the heart of federalism, will be real at last. No longer will centralizing governments be able to steal the decisions that properly belong locally.

Volunteering is predicted to grow, offering more opportunities for part-time participation in the local community. Governments will start to rely more heavily on the institutions of what is called the Civil Society to provide support and advice. They may promote it as opportunity for good citizenship, but the move will be driven, as ever, by economics. It will be cheaper, as well as (possibly) better, if done for almost free by local enthusiasts and people of goodwill. Never mind the motive, it will all help to bond our communities together. I have been struck recently by how many of my newly-retired friends are acting as drivers for the old or disabled who need to be taken to hospitals or appointments. 'I get to talk to some fascinating characters,' they always say, neighbours whom they would never have met otherwise.

Sadly, even this more hopeful view of the future won't necessarily be all roses. Left to ourselves we may seek to create our own communities of choice, of people like us. If we leave it at that, however, full of goodwill though we may be we will not automatically bump into people who aren't like us. Society could still fragment, with fewer national themes around which to coalesce. That elusive but crucial glue of society, social capital, could erode. Fear, suspicion and intolerance could grow. Racialism, ageism and tribalism could grow. Goodbye then to live-and-let-live.

Which way will it go? The omens are not all good.

I recall my optimistic hopes for society, back in 1981.

I used to think that as societies got richer they would quieten down. Instead they seem to have got more frenetic. I used to think that wealth would make people nicer and more tolerant. Instead they became more competitive and more protective of what they had. I had hoped that instead of some having too much work and too little leisure, while others had the reverse, it would all get evened out. Whereas our parents worked 100,000 hours in a lifetime, our children, I forecast, would need to work only half of that because of increased productivity. I was naive. Most preferred more money to more leisure and went on working the 100,000 hours if they could.

Economic progress seems only to have raised the stakes in life's horse race, not levelled the handicaps. There were two sorts of justice, I emphasized back then, the justice that gives everyone what they deserve, and the other sort, that gives them what they need. The first is only tolerable if the latter is seen to be met. That is a job that only government can do. For too long the British and the Americans have concentrated on that first type of justice.

Non-selective comprehensive state education was meant to give everyone in Britain an equal chance in life. It didn't, because it wasn't able to take into account the fact that every young person is different, with their individual talents, different aspirations and their own ways of learning. We are getting better now at providing different courses for particular horses, but there is still a long way to go. This, too, is largely a task for government.

I had hoped, back then, that the emerging technologies would allow many more people to work from home, thus recreating communities of place, the kind of inclusive communities of the agricultural age. I didn't want such communities for myself, but I thought that others would. I was wrong. Most people still hankered for the community of interest, the work community, and the physical space and physical contiguity that it offered. This is changing slowly, but the new homeworkers use the technology not to enable themselves to be local but, instead, to interact globally, locking themselves in their homes rather than bonding with the neighbours.

Twenty years ago words like ecology and organic began to appear. Rachel Carson's book *Silent Spring* had alerted the world to a looming catastrophe. I watched hopefully as Earth Summits were followed by protocols and agreements and ever more international meetings. Today, we continue to hear of the threats to the environment, of forests disappearing, of seas and temperatures rising, but few seem to be concerned enough to take action. How can one person change the world, they ask, and pass by.

Finally, I had hoped that the increasing interest in the spiritual life would lead to a more caring society, one that reached out to those on the margins. I had looked to it for a way out of our dilemmas. Instead, the new spirituality seems to be more inwardly focused, looking for personal salvation or renewal, withdrawing from engagement with outsiders instead of seeking it. It is not religion as I knew it.

I had not realized how steeped I was in the Christian tradition until I heard the tale that the chaplain to the English church in Florence told me. He was showing a group of American college students around the Uffizi Gallery, drawing their attention to the many lovely Madonnas there, amongst other things. At the end of the tour he heard one young woman say to another, 'Have you noticed, it's so typical – it's always a boy baby that she's holding?'

We laughed. Then we paused. Was this what a secular society meant, one without even the stories of religion to bind the culture, to underpin the morality? Have we underrated the importance of the Christian culture, as distinct from the Christian religion, in Western society? Can a society survive, we wondered, without such a set of stories, a common framework of understood morality and a shared understanding of what it means to be human, without a religion and without a god?

Maybe the problem is that there are too many gods today. Carlos Efferson, the American philosopher poet, believes so. At the head of his list are still the Gods of Holy Books and Sacred Rights, although their worshippers are dwindling. Becoming more important today, however, are the Gods of Power, or Pride, or Work or Wealth – Gods who divide men rather than unite them. He might have added a few more – the Gods of Fame or Fashion, for instance. Then, he says, there are those whose God is themselves, who 'are always at the altar of their own wants, certain that this is the way that life should be lived, and that those who don't agree are fools'. There are Tribal Gods, whose followers believe that wrong has been done them, 'and the fuel of their hearts is that those who did the wrong must suffer pain'. Lastly there are those in great numbers who claim no god at all.

I recognize the world that Carlos Efferson is describing and my heart sinks. If these various gods are what passes for religion today, they will only add to our problems not solve them. We have become like the Greeks of old, with a god for every whim and every season, gods who fought each other, gods who divided the people rather than united them. Have our traditional religions nothing better to offer?

If we are honest, religion bonded society through fear not love. Religion laid down commandments, set standards and devised punishments; in the case of Christianity they ranged from the terrors of the Inquisition to the recital of Hail Marys. Every religion had its own varieties of dos and don'ts, its own set of penalties. As long as the bulk of the people believed in the underlying premise it worked, society obeyed.

That underlying premise is no longer accepted in a modern secular society. Religion has become an affair of sects, many of them verging on idolatry. They have their enthusiastic followers but, as Carlos Efferson declares, they are each worshipping just one god amongst many, they can no longer dictate to society. Instead, governments begin to move into the empty space, trying to spell out what a good life is, what makes a family, what to eat or not to eat, to smoke or not to smoke, at what age to have sex, even how to behave to our fellow humans of a different race, religion or gender. We reject the emerging nanny state but have nothing to put in its place, no other way of arriving at a set of norms and standards. Could we, I wonder, reinvent religion for a modern age?

I am not a Christian in the conventional sense. I once received a prize, awarded at Lambeth Palace, for a programme that I had made about my religious journey in life. The citation gave the game away: 'a well-made and thought-provoking programme despite the presenter's unorthodox view of Christianity.'

I do not believe in a personal god. Perhaps it is a continuing reaction against my childhood, but the idea of a Supreme Being intervening in the universe is repugnant to me. Having said that I do believe that the Christian story, along with the Jewish, Buddhist, Muslim and Hindu stories, has much to tell us about our human condition and the meaning of life. If I knew more about other religions I suspect that it might be true of them as well. They are stories, however, not history, myths in the true sense of that word, ways of proclaiming important truths about individuals and societies in times when people thought in particulars not in abstracts, in stories with meanings, in pictures with a message.

They had power, those stories. They inspired great music and wonderful art, magnificent literature. They gave people the courage to fight great battles for great causes, to endure great afflictions, even suffer death. True, they also drove people to commit horrendous crimes when those people appropriated religion for their own tribal purposes. What is it that makes people so willing to kill and be killed for something they cannot see or count?

We would be crazy to abandon something so powerful, but it does need reinterpretation for our day and age. The Christian concepts of new life after death, of redemption and forgiveness, of the crucial importance of unconditional love, all resonate today. For resurrection, for instance, read reinvention, the need to find a new life when the old one ends or falters and the need to believe that you have the power and the ability do it, but *now*, in this world, not later in some world beyond the stars. Forgiveness, too, is crucial to growth. If you can't forgive your enemies you are stuck with them for ever. It can be even more difficult at times to forgive oneself. Religion had ways of dealing with this block, through confession and absolution. In their place we now use therapists.

My personal way of reinterpretation is to find my own synonyms for God, such as Good and Truth. I reinterpret the idea that God is to be looked for in us, by holding that there is good in all of us, as well as evil, and that one purpose of life is to surface the good and contain the evil, in ourselves but also in others. I see life as a continuing search for the truth in myself, by which I mean living with my own conscience, being what I could be rather than what I can get away with. I know only too well when I am living a lie, courting popularity, or ducking out of the implications of what I know to be true. It is back to Marsilio Ficino and the Italian Renaissance and his idea that our soul is that which is greatest within us, our possibility.

I also go back to a much more pragmatic figure – 'Capability' Brown, the landscape architect who designed so many of the parklands that surround England's great houses. He was nicknamed Capability because he was apt to observe, as he surveyed a landscape that he had been asked to transform: 'It's got a lot of capability', by which he meant a lot of potential. I would not mind being called Capability Charles if it meant that there was a lot of potential there waiting to be developed, potential for good, of course. It isn't easy. A friend was once asked, 'Don't you get tired of being you?' It's a good question. It is tempting to escape from oneself at times.

My belief in the long search for my latent 'capability' sustains me. I recognize, however, that it is a religion for a flea, that it is not going to unite a people, nor lead to great crusades or mighty reforms. I would like 'capability' to be the core of a humane society, but it needs to be accompanied by another culture, one that focuses on a concern for others. To balance the morality of self-interest, however enlightened that self-interest may be, there needs to be another morality of concern for our fellows, the commandment to love your neighbour as yourself that Christianity has preached down the ages. The growing concern for legislation on human rights is an expression of that concern, but laws, to be effective, need to be backed by a moral consensus. In saying this, I am conscious of the famous words inscribed on Karl Marx's tomb in Highgate cemetery, which may have been by way of apology for his own life: 'Philosophers have only interpreted the world. The point is, however, to change it.'

Would that we could.

All that I can do, all that most of us can do, perhaps, is to live life the way we think that it ought to be lived. It is twenty years since my life changed to that of a flea. In twenty years' time, if I survive that long, I shall be nearly ninety. There is a sealed letter in my files addressed to my children, to be opened after my death. It contains mundane details of my affairs, but also my thoughts on life's priorities for myself, something I wish I had discussed with my own father before he died. I update the letter occasionally and reflect on what I have said in earlier versions. It has changed, I note, over the years, as ambition fades and life acquires new and gentler tones.

Meanwhile, there is an old Chinese saying that 'Happiness is having something to do, something to hope for and someone to love.' I plan to be happy.

INDEX

ABOUT THE AUTHOR

Charles Handy is a London-based author and broadcaster whose books have sold more than a million copies worldwide. He describes himself as a social philosopher, writing about the changes in work and society that affect all our lives and organizations. A Fellow of the London Business School, he has been a regular commentator on the BBC and a consultant to a wide variety of organizations in business, government, education, and health.

Harvard Business School Press has published Handy's *The Elephant and the Flea*, *Beyond Certainty*, *The Age of Paradox*, and *The Age of Unreason*. His other books include *Understanding Organizations*, *Gods of Management*, *The Future of Work*, and *The Making of Managers*.